PEACE AND STABILITY IN THE ASIA PACIFIC REGION:
ASSESSMENT OF THE SECURITY ARCHITECTURE

PEACE AND STABILITY IN THE ASIA PACIFIC REGION:
ASSESSMENT OF THE SECURITY ARCHITECTURE

Edited By
Maj Gen Y K Gera (Retd)

BASED ON PROCEEDINGS OF
NATIONAL SECURITY SEMINAR 2011
HELD AT USI, NEW DELHI
ON 17-18 NOV 2011

(Established 1870)

United Service Institution of India
New Delhi

Vij Books India Pvt Ltd
New Delhi (India)

Published by

Vij Books India Pvt Ltd
(Publishers, Distributors & Importers)
2/19, Ansari Road, Darya Ganj
New Delhi - 110002
Phones: 91-11-43596460, 91-11- 65449971
Fax: 91-11-47340674
e-mail : vijbooks@rediffmail.com
web: www.vijbooks.com

Copyright © 2012, United Service Institution of India, New Delhi

ISBN: 978-93-81411-30-8

Price in India: ₹ 995/-
Price outside India: US $ 45

All rights reserved.

No part of this book may be reproduced, stored in a retrieval system, transmitted or utilised in any form or by any means, electronic, mechanical, photocopying, recording or otherwise, without the prior permission of the copyright owner. Applications for such permission should be addressed to the publisher.

The views expressed in the book are of authors/contributors and not necessarily those of the USI or publishers.

Printed in India
at Narula Printers

CONTENTS

Concept Note		IX
Participants		X
Acronyms		XXXI
Inaugural Session		1
Welcome Address	Vice Admiral Shekhar Sinha, AVSM, NM & Bar, CISC and President, USI Council.	3
Keynote Address	Admiral Nirmal Verma, PVSM, AVSM, ADC, Chairman COSC and Chief of the Naval Staff.	9
Special Addresses	Lieutenant General Tran Thai Binh, IDS, Vietnam. Lieutenant General Bang, Hyo-Bok (Retd), KIDA, RoK.	15
First Session	**Strategic and Security Environment in the Asia Pacific Region.**	19
Auditorium		21
Chairman	Shri SK Bhutani, IFS (Retd).	
First Paper	Professor Zhao Gancheng, SIIS, China.	22
Second Paper	Mr Tetsuo Kotani, Okazaki Institute, Japan.	35
Third Paper	Dr Michael Pillsbury, DOD, USA.	46
Seminar Room 1		53
Chairman	Mr Fyodor Lukyanov, Editor-in-Chief, Russia, in Global Affairs.	
First Paper	Professor Bharat Karnad, CPR.	54
Second Paper	Sr. Col Tran Hau Hung, IDIR, Vietnam.	68
Third Paper	Ambassador Andrea Perugini, MOFA, Italy.	73

Discussion	Centralised in Auditorium	80
Second Session	**Existing Political and Economic Frameworks in the Asia Pacific-Have They Fulfilled Regional Aspirations?**	89
Auditorium		91
Chairman	Rear Admiral Sumihiko Kawamura, Okazaki Institute, Japan.	
First Paper	Dr Man-Jung Mignonne Chan, Prospect Foundation, Taiwan.	92
Second Paper	Lieutenant General PC Katoch, PVSM, UYSM, AVSM,SC (Retd)	97
Third Paper	Sr Col Vu Van Khanh, IDS, Vietnam.	112
Seminar Room 1		116
Chairman	Professor Richard Rigby, ANU, Australia.	
First Paper	Mr Hideki Asari, JIIA, Japan.	117
Second Paper	Professor Moon Jangnyeol, RINSA, South Korea.	121
Third Paper	Dr Claudia Astarita, CeMiSS, Italy.	129
Discussion	Centralised in Auditorium	146
Third Session	**Building an Enduring Security Architecture for the Asia Pacific Region.**	153
Auditorium		154
Chairman	Lieutenant General Vinay Shankar, PVSM, AVSM,VSM (Retd).	
First Paper	Professor Su Hao, CFAU,China.	155
Second Paper	Professor Richard Rigby and Dr. Brendan Taylor, ANU, Australia.	158

CONTENTS

Third Paper	Dr. Andrew C. Winner, NWC, USA.	161
Seminar Room 1		**168**
Chairman	Shri Ranjit Singh Kalha, IFS (Retd).	
First Paper	Professor Swaran Singh, JNU.	169
Second Paper	Dr Kim Changsu, KIDA, South Korea.	177
Third Paper	Mr Fyodor Lukyanov, Editor-in-Chief, *Russia in Global Affairs*.	179
Discussion	Centralised in Auditorium	182
Valedictory Session		**189**
Valedictory Address	Shri Ranjan Mathai, IFS, Foreign Secretary.	191
Vote of Thanks	Lieutenant General PK Singh, PVSM, AVSM (Retd), Director, USI.	197

CONCEPT NOTE

Peace and Stability in the Asia-Pacific Region: Assessment of the Security Architecture

As defined by the United Nations Educational Scientific and Cultural Organisation (UNESCO), 48 countries constitute the Asia Pacific region. While the list includes India, Australia, Japan, South Korea, Taiwan and China, it excludes the US. However, in the current strategic discourse, Asia Pacific generally includes the countries of the Pacific Rim, including the USA and Australia, South Asia, SE Asia, East Asia and NE Asia. India, which essentially is an Asian, South Asian and an Indian Ocean entity, is firmly categorised now as a leading power in the Asia Pacific, along with China, Japan, South Korea, Indonesia, Vietnam, Singapore and Taiwan, among the others in the Pacific Rim. It is also noteworthy that the Asia Pacific region consists of nearly 4 billion people out of the world's 7 billion and accounts for nearly 60 per cent of the global GDP. By 2020, seven of the world's ten leading economies are likely to be in the Asia Pacific region.

The United Nations, recognising the growing importance of this region set-up the ESCAP, namely, the UN Economic and Social Commission for Asia and the Pacific. Even at the height of the economic crisis that the world endured a couple of years back, this remained the fastest growing region globally, averaging an overall 7 per cent growth, with China growing at 9.5 and India at 8.5 per cent in 2010, respectively. Almost 50 per cent of the world's maritime trade passes through the confined straits and chokepoints in the archipelagic waters of Southeast Asia and the South China Sea. Thus, this region, which is of vital economic significance for the entire world, lends itself not only to newer forms of regional and global rivalry but also varied forms of traditional and non-traditional security threats like maritime terrorism, sea piracy, poaching, access to territorial waters and so on.

This region is also witness to dozens of outstanding and potentially dangerous territorial disputes. The Asia Pacific could also become an arena for the new cold war with an emerging and consequently assertive China taking head-on the sole superpower, the USA, now somewhat weary and over-stretched with its global commitments and interventions in Iraq and Afghanistan. Some analysts feel that the world's maritime future is likely to be determined in large measure in the Asia Pacific, particularly by the developing relationship between the maritime powers of the area.

Growing democracy and political pluralism have created a seemingly stable and prosperous environment. Clandestine nuclear programs, border and territorial disputes, sovereignty claims and counter claims, piracy, transnational terrorism and extremism are a few problems that have plagued the region. While strategists across the board remain wary of a monolithic Asia Pacific, they are in unison about the fact that this emerging and important region needs better regional and international mechanisms and security arrangements as well.

Global affairs today are traversing through a period of instability. The reason for this instability lies in the transition of global power that is currently underway. The two poles to this transition are the relative decline of the United States and the rise of China. While the US's relative decline has been a long and slow process, the evident and more dramatic rise of China over the last two decades is going to impact not just its neighbours in the Asia Pacific, but in the entire world.

History has shown us that great powers will always seek to dominate their neighbourhood and as much of the rest of the world as they can. There is nothing peculiarly Chinese, Indian or Korean about it. But the obverse is equally true. The rise of the Asia Pacific giants is likely to be as problematic, tense and destabilising as that of any other powers.

Asia Pacific states have tended to follow traditional approaches to their security policies. While there have been some attempts to forge multilateral alliances, most nations have sought either bilateral alliances or their own security mechanisms, to secure their national and security interests. However, since the mid-1990s, this approach seems to have given way to an enthusiasm for multinational cooperation. This has led to the creation of new institutions with security cooperation as their main purpose. In addition, new groupings appear to be fostering wide ranging policy cooperation, where security sits alongside other policy issues, such as trade, investment and culture. Existing institutions and mechanisms have also started including security on their agendas.

Despite a shift to multilateral and a more prominent institutional approach, the Asia Pacific states are known to base their regional strategies on traditional military means. Majority of the security cooperation arrangements in the Asia Pacific are through bilateral alliances or the quasi-alliance arrangements that the US has with many states in the region. The United States of America's forward military power projection and bilateral alliances and security partnerships provide the most significant force stabilising the region's current order. This architecture that has found favour with the Asia Pacific states has been a predominant mechanism since 2000. This trend shows that countries have highly flexible regional security policies and they lack confidence in multilateralism. The US, on its part, has avoided reliance on multilateral approach in the Asia Pacific whereas it manages its European security engagement through NATO.

Globalisation is prompting a broader reconsideration of the utility of cooperation through multilateral means. While the need of the hour is effective cooperation, the continuation of bilateral approaches, together with strategic competition in the Asia Pacific's security setting, needs to be reviewed objectively.

This seminar intends to examine the current state and possible future trajectory of efforts to create an Asia Pacific security architecture. The problems are challenging but not insurmountable. Efforts to build an appropriate security architecture would be in the interest of the region.

PARTICIPANTS

Lieutenant General PK Singh, PVSM, AVSM (Retd)

Lieutenant General PK Singh, is the Director of the United Service Institution of India, New Delhi, since 1st January 2009. During his military career, spanning 41 years, he participated in active counter-insurgency operations and the Indo-Pak War of 1971. He retired from active service in September 2008 as C-in-C (Army Commander). His academic qualifications include M Sc, M Phil and a Post Graduate Diploma in Business Management. He is a Council Member of the Indian Council of World Affairs, a member of the International Advisory Board, RUSI International, UK and Advisor to the Fair Observer, USA.

Admiral Nirmal Verma, PVSM, AVSM, ADC

Admiral Nirmal Verma assumed command of the Indian Navy on 31 August 2009 as the twentieth Chief of the Naval Staff. He became the Chairman, Chiefs of Staff Committee, on 31 July 2011.

A specialist in Communication and Electronic Warfare, Admiral Verma has had an illustrious four-decade career during which he held important Command and force-development assignments. He commanded INS Udaygiri, a Leander Class Frigate; INS Ranvir, a Kashin Class Destroyer and INS Viraat, the Aircraft Carrier. He was involved closely in shaping the future Indian military leadership while commanding the Indian Naval Academy at Goa and during his appointments as Head of the Naval Training Team at the Defence Services Staff College, Wellington, and Senior Directing Staff (Navy), at the National Defence College, New Delhi.

His overseas experiences include a stint in the former Soviet Union as part of the commissioning crew of the first Indian Kashin Class Destroyer; attending the Staff Course at the Royal Navy Staff College, Greenwich, UK and the Naval Command Course at the US Naval War College, Newport,

Rhode Island.

After assuming Flag Rank, Admiral Verma has been closely associated with the growth, consolidation and modernisation of the Indian Navy and its operational commands. As a Rear Admiral, he was Chief of Staff of the Eastern Naval Command; Flag Officer Commanding Maharashtra Naval Area and Assistant Chief of Naval Staff (Policy and Plans). As a Vice Admiral, he held three apex-level leadership positions – first as the Chief of Personnel, when he led the human resource development endeavour of the Navy; then as Vice Chief of the Naval Staff when he directed and oversaw programs to enhance the Navy's combat capabilities and infrastructure and finally as the Flag Officer Commanding-in-Chief, Eastern Naval Command, when he provided vision and vigour to maritime and coastal security on the Eastern Seaboard.

Vice Admiral Shekhar Sinha, AVSM, NM & BAR

Vice Admiral Shekhar Sinha, AVSM, NM and Bar was commissioned on 01 June 1974 into Naval Aviation Fighter Stream. He was awarded the Pronobe De Trophy for standing first during the Operational flying Training. He graduated as Flying Instructor from FIS, Tambaram and instructed on Kiran aircraft at Air Force Academy. He has flown over 2700 hrs on 18 different types of aircrafts, mostly from aircraft carrier Vikrant and Viraat on the Sea Harrier. He has held command of two Sea Harrier Squadrons and the air station at Goa.

During the long naval career, the Flag Officer has commanded the Coast Guard Ship Ranijindan (during Op – Pawan), IN Ships Saryu, Shakti and Missile Destroyer Delhi. He was the Fleet Operations Officer of Western Fleet during Op – Parakram.

In the Flag rank, he has held appointments of Flag Officer Naval Aviation, Flag Officer Commanding Goa Area and Assistant Chief of Naval Staff (Air). He has also held the command of the sword arm of the Navy – the Western Fleet.

Vice Admiral Shekhar Sinha is alumnus of the Defence Services Staff College, College of Naval Warfare and National Defence College. The

Flag officer is a recipient of Ati Vishisht Seva Medal and two gallantry awards Nau Sena Medal & Bar.

On promotion to the rank of Vice Admiral, he served as the Controller Personnel Services at IHQ/MoD (Navy), Deputy Chief of Integrated Defence Staff Operations and Policy Planning Force Development at HQ IDS, New Delhi.

Vice Admiral Shekhar Sinha assumed the duties of CISC, on 29 April 2011.

Lieutenant General Tran Thai Binh, PhD

He joined the Vietnam People's Army in 1971. As a Colonel, he was Vice Commanding Officer, COS of Infantry Division No. 3, Army Corps No 4. He served as Associate Professor in the National Defence Academy (NDA). As a Major General, he was Director of Department of Education and Training, NDA and later on he became the Vice Chairman. Since 2008, he is Director General of the Institute for Defence Strategy, Ministry of National Defence.

Shri SK Bhutani, IFS (Retd)

Sudarshan Bhutani joined Indian Foreign Service in 1955 at the age of 22. After training in India and a year in Oxford, he did a yearlong course at Beijing University while working at the Indian Embassy. He spent over fifteen years in the Asia-Pacific region. He was Chairman-cum-Secretary General of the International Commission for Supervision and Control in Vietnam, Ambassador to Indonesia and High Commissioner to Australia.

His other area of interest is the Arab world. As joint secretary in the Ministry, after the 1973 Arab-Israeli War and ensuing energy crisis, he handled political relations with all countries from Afghanistan to Morocco. He was Ambassador in Egypt in the late nineteen eighties.

His other assignments included Consul-General of India for the Western United States based in San Francisco, Ambassador of India to Poland and to Portugal.

After retirement, he continues to take active interest in current national security issues. He has written articles in specialised journals and authored a book on India's relations with China, titled '*A Clash of Political Cultures, Sino-Indian Relations 1957-62*', which was published in January 2004.

Professor Zhao Gancheng

Professor Zhao Gancheng, senior fellow and director of South Asia Studies, Shanghai Institutes for International Studies (SIIS), joined the SIIS in 1985. Earlier, he focussed on European Studies as research assistant, research fellow, deputy director and director. As a senior fellow and director of South Asia Studies at SIIS, his focus is on Indian politics and diplomacy, China-India relations and South Asia regional security. A large number of articles authored by him have been published in a number of Chinese and foreign journals. Zhao Gancheng graduated in majored in english from Shanghai Foreign Language College and got his masters degree from the School of Advanced International Studies, the Johns Hopkins University of the United States.

Mr Tetsuo Kotani

Mr Tetsuo Kotani is a Special Research Fellow at the Okazaki Institute in Tokyo. He is also a senior research fellow at the Research Institute for Peace and Security (RIPS) in Tokyo, a member of the International Advisory Board at Project 2049 Institute in Washington and a nonresident SPF fellow at Pacific Forum, CSIS, in Honolulu. He was a research fellow at Ocean Policy Research Foundation (OPRF) in 2006-2010. His dissertation focus is on the strategic implications of homeporting US carriers in Japan. His other research interests include US-Japan relations and international relations and maritime security in the Asia-Pacific region. He has authored a large number of articles, some of which have been published in English. He was a visiting fellow at the US-Japan Centre at Vanderbilt University. He received a security studies fellowship from the Research Institute for Peace and Security (RIPS), 2006-2008. He won the 2003 Japanese Defence Minister Prize.

Dr Michael Pillsbury

Born in California in 1945, Pillsbury was educated at Stanford University (B.A. in History with Honours in Social Thought) and Columbia University (M.A., Ph.D.). Major academic advisers to Pillsbury at Columbia were Zbigniew Brzezinski and Michel Oksenberg, who later played key roles in the Jimmy Carter administration, on policy towards both China and Afghanistan. Pillsbury studied the art and practice of bureaucratic politics with Roger Hilsman, President John Kennedy's intelligence director at the State Department and the author of 'Politics Of Policy Making In Defence and Foreign Affairs'. At Stanford, Pillsbury's academic mentor was Mark Mancall, author of two books on the influence of ancient traditions on Chinese foreign policy.

In 1969-1970, Pillsbury was the Assistant Political Affairs Officer at the United Nations. From 1971-72, he was a doctoral dissertation Fellow for the National Science Foundation in Taiwan and in 1973-1977, Pillsbury was an analyst at the Social Science Department at RAND. In 1978, Pillsbury was a research fellow at the Centre for Science and International Affairs at Harvard University.

During the Reagan administration, Dr. Pillsbury was the Assistant Under Secretary of Defence for Policy Planning and responsible for implementation of the program of covert aid known as the Reagan Doctrine. In 1975-76, while an analyst at the RAND Corporation, Pillsbury published articles in Foreign Policy and International Security, recommending that the United States establish intelligence and military ties with China. The proposal, publicly commended by Ronald Reagan, Henry Kissinger and James Schlesinger, later became US policy during the Carter and Reagan administrations.

Mr Fyodor Lukyanov

Fyodor Lukyanov is Editor-in-Chief of the *Russia in Global Affairs* journal published in Russian and English. As head of *Russia in Global Affairs* since its founding in 2002, he greatly contributed towards making this journal Russia's most authoritative source of expert opinion on Russian foreign policy. Mr. Lukyanov worked for Russian and international media from

1990 to 2002, as a commentator on international affairs. He is now contributing to different media in the US, Europe and China. His monthly "Geopolitics" column appears in the Russian edition of Forbes magazine and weekly foreign policy column is published in RIA Novosti web-edition. His articles appeared in academic journals like Social Research, Europe-Asia Studies, Columbia Journal of International Affairs, Limes. He is a member of the Presidium of Council on Foreign and Defence Policy, an independent organisation providing foreign policy expertise. He is a member of Presidential Council on Human Rights and Russian Council on Foreign Relations. Fyodor Lukyanov holds a degree in Germanic Languages from Moscow State University.

Professor Bharat Karnad

Bharat Karnad is a Research Professor in National Security Studies at the Centre for Policy Research, New Delhi. He is the author of *India's Nuclear Policy* [Praeger, 2008], *Nuclear Weapons and Indian Security: The Realist Foundations of Strategy* and author-editor of *Future Imperiled: India's Security in the 1990s and Beyond* [Viking-Penguin India, 1994]. He was a Member of the National Security Advisory Board, National Security Council, Government of India and Member of the Nuclear Doctrine Drafting Group and formerly Advisor, Defence Expenditure to the Finance Commission, India. He is a regular lecturer at military training institutions and forums and conducts an annual Strategic Nuclear Orientation Course for senior armed forces officers for the Integrated Defence Staff, Ministry of Defence.

Ambassador Andrea Perugini

He is a career diplomat and is Deputy Director General/Principal Director for Asia, Oceania and the Pacific, Directorate General for Globalisation and for Asia, Sub-Saharan Africa and Latin America. Prior to this, he served as Deputy to the Director General for Asia, Oceania, the Pacific & Antarctica. He has been ambassador of Italy to Vietnam from July 2008 to December 2010. His earlier diplomatic assignments include Coordinator on European Unions internal market and Lisbon strategy on growth and employment at the Directorate General for European interaction, Italian Ministry of Foreign Affairs; head of office on economic affairs and European Union sectoral policies, First Counsellor at the Permanent Delegation of Italy to the OECD (Organisation for Economic Cooperation and Development) in Paris, with focus on financial Action Task Force Activities and fight against corruption of public officials in international economic transactions, health, transportation, education and investment promotion sectors.

Rear Admiral Sumihiko Kawamura (Retd)

Rear Admiral Sumihiko Kawamura graduated from the Japanese National Defence Academy in 1960. He is a naval aviator. He attended the Staff College course.

In addition to approximately 6,000 flight hours on patrol aircraft, he has held a number of staff and command appointments, including three years as Naval Attache in the Embassy of Japan in Washington, D.C.

Since retiring from the Japanese Maritime Self Defence Force (JMSDF) in 1991, he has frequently appeared in the Japanese media as a commentator on maritime and security issues. In 1998, he established the Kawamura Institute for Maritime and Strategic Studies. Since 2002, Admiral Kawamura has served concurrently as Vice President of the Okazaki Institute, headed by Ambassador Hisahiko Okazaki and promoted strategic studies and security dialogue with overseas counterparts.

Ms Mignonne Man-Jung Chan

Dr Chan is Executive Director of the Chinese Taipei APEC Study Centre, and Senior Lecturer at the Foreign Service Institute. In addition, she serves as Group Leader of the Global Business Unit at the Prospect Foundation, Group Leader of Economic Security Unit at the Centre for Strategic Study, Institute of International Relations, National Chengchi University.

Dr Chan served as Senior Advisor to the President at the National Security Council between May 2008 and May 2010. She was appointed Director General of PECC International Secretariat from July 1999 to

December 2001. Prior to her PECC appointment, she served as Director (Research & Analysis) at the APEC Secretariat in Singapore. She was Director & Research Associate of the International Affairs Division in Taiwan Institute of Economic Research (TIER) for 6 years.

Lieutenant General PC Katoch, PVSM, UYSM, AVSM, SC (Retd)

Lieutenant General PC Katoch, PVSM, UYSM, AVSM, SC, superannuated as Director General Information Systems of Indian Army in 2009. He fought in the 1971 India-Pakistan War, commanded an independent commando company in insurgency areas, a Special Forces Battalion under the IPKF in Sri Lanka, a Brigade on Siachen Glacier, a Division in Ladakh and a Strike Corps in South Western Theatre. He represented India at the International Sky Diving Competition at USSR in 1976, served as Defence Attache in Japan with accreditation to Republic of Korea. A Master in Defence Studies, he is an alumni of the Defence Services Staff College, Senior and Higher Command Courses and National Defence College. A former Colonel of The Parachute Regiment, he has extensive experience of operations in mountains, high altitude, deserts, counter insurgency and counter terrorism. Post retirement, he has authored over 70 articles on military, security, topical and technical issues. He is member of the USI Council and active participant in seminars at national and international levels. He chaired an international seminar on Leadership at Maldives in 2009, was part of the fourth round of Afghanistan-India-Pakistan Trialogue held at Kabul in 2010, presented a paper on Counter Terrosism at PACOM, Hawaii, during 2011 and was part of the USI delegation to China in 2011.

Senior Colonel Vu Van Khanh

Senior Colonel Vu Van Khanh was born in Thai Binh Province, Vietnam in 1960. In December 1983, he joined the Vietnam People's Army. He worked at the Department of Military Science, Chemical Corps from December 1983 to October 1995. In November 1995, he was selected as an information officer for the Information Centre for Military Science and Technology at the Ministry of Defence. He completed his BA in Press and Publication at the University of Press. From September 1999 to January 2000, he attended the Command and Staff Course at the Army Academy in Da Lat, Vietnam.

From January to December 2008, he did the Defence and Strategic Studies Course, Post Graduate Diploma in Strategic Studies, Centre for Defence and Strategic Studies (CDSS), Australian Defence College and completed the Master of Arts Program in Strategic Studies at Deakin University, Australia.

From February 2000 to June 2004, he worked as a journalist and editor of the Military Science Review. He was appointed as Deputy Editor-in-Chief of the Military Science Review in July 2004. In May 2005, he was selected as a researcher at the Institute for Defence Strategy and later became Deputy Director of the Department of International Relations Studies, Institute for Defence Strategy, Ministry of National Defence.

Professor Richard Rigby

Richard Rigby graduated with First Class Honours in History from the ANU in 1970 and went on to do his PhD.

Richard joined Australia's Department of Foreign Affairs in 1975, where he worked until the end of 2001. His postings included Tokyo, Beijing (twice), Shanghai, London and Israel (Ambassador, 2000-2001). He then joined the Office of National Assessments as Assistant Director-General, responsible for North and South Asia, where he worked until taking up his current position with the ANU China Institute in April 2008.

While engaged in government work, Richard continued to pursue his academic interests with a series of translations, book reviews and articles on China-related topics. His personal interests in Chinese studies are primarily literary and historical but his profession has ensured a thorough immersion in all aspects of contemporary China and other major Asian cultures.

Mr. Hideki Asari

Hideki Asari graduated from School of Economics, Waseda University, Tokyo, Japan in 1986 and joined Ministry of Foreign Affairs of Japan. He did his MA in Philosophy, Politics and Economics from University of Oxford, UK in 1987. He has served in Economic Affairs Bureau, Treaties Bureau and Economic Cooperation Bureau, MOFA. He has had a tenure as First

Secretary, Embassy of Japan, Republic of Korea. Currently he is Deputy Director-General, Japan Institute of International Affairs.

Professor Moon Jangnyeol

Moon Jangnyeol is an associate professor in the department of military strategy in Korea National Defence University (KNDU). He graduated from Korea military academy in 1982 and earned his PhD degree in physics from Purdue University in 1991. After teaching Physics for some years at the third Korea military academy, he moved to the arms control office under the ministry of national defence in 1996 and then to Korea national defence university in 1999. During 2003 and 2004, he served as a strategic planning officer in the secretariat of the national security council. His teaching and research areas include: military strategy and weapons systems, science and technology policy, information and cyber warfare, and peace and unification matters of the Korean peninsula.

Ms Claudia Astarita

Ms Claudia Astarita was born on 17 Jun 1979. She did her doctorate on "Sino-Indian Relations : Political and Economic Implications" from University of Hong Kong. She researches on India, China and Korea, has authored two books and writes in journals. She has also been a journalist and has taught at John Cabot University and Bologna University. Since April 2011, she is affiliated to Centre for Military and Strategic Studies (CeMISS), Rome.

Lieutenant General Vinay Shankar, PVSM, AVSM, VSM (Retd)

He was commissioned in the Regiment of Artillery in June 1960. He attended prestigious courses like Defence Services Staff College (DSSC), Higher Command and National Defence College (NDC).

He took part in 1962, 1965, 1971 operations. Lt Gen Vinay Shankar is an accomplished army aviator. He served in the counter insurgency area of Nagaland. He held various appointments at Army Headquarters – DDG(SD), Dy MS, ADG (WE), DG (D&CW) and retired as DG (Arty).

At present, he is one of the Council Members of the United Service Institution of India.

Dr Su Hao

Dr. Su Hao is a professor in the Department of Diplomacy at the China Foreign Affairs University (CFAU) and director of Centre for Strategic and Conflict Management. He is also affiliated to some institutions in China, such as, President of Beijing Association of Geo-strategy and Development, China Association of Asian-African Development Exchange and China Association of China-ASEAN. He got his B.A. in History and M.A. in International Relations from Beijing Normal University and Ph. D. in International Relations from China Foreign Affairs University. He did advanced study in the School of Oriental and African Studies, University of London in 1993-1995; and was a Fulbright scholar in Columbia University and University of California at Berkeley in 2001-2002.

Dr Brendan Taylor

Dr Brendan Taylor is Senior Lecturer and Director of Graduate Studies at the Strategic and Defence Studies Centre, Australian National University. He is a specialist on Korean Peninsula security issues, great power strategic relations in the Asia-Pacific, economic sanctions and Asian security architecture. His publications have featured in leading international journals: International Affairs, Survival, Asian Security, Review of International Studies and the Australian Journal of International Affairs. He is the author of *Sanctions as Grand Strategy*, which was recently published in the International Institute for Strategic Studies (IISS) Adelphi book series, as well as American Sanctions in the Asia Pacific (Routledge, 2010).

Professor Andrew C. Winner

Andrew C. Winner is a Professor of Strategic Studies in the Strategic Research Department at the Naval War College, Newport, Rhode Island. His areas of focus are South Asia, nonproliferation, maritime partnerships, maritime strategy, the Middle East, and US national security. He is chairman of the Indian Ocean Studies Group at the Naval War College. In June 2007, he was awarded the Navy Meritorious Civilian Service Award for his work on the Navy's new maritime strategy. Prior to his current appointment, he was a senior staff member at the Institute for Foreign Policy Analysis. Prior to joining the Institute, he held various positions at the U.S. Department of State on the staff of the Under Secretary of State for Arms Control and International Security Affairs and in the Bureau of Political-Military Affairs where he worked on nonproliferation, security in the Persian Gulf, arms transfer policy, NATO enlargement and security assistance. He is the co-author of Indian Naval Strategy in the 21st Century, Routledge, 2009. He holds a Ph.D. from the University of Maryland, College Park, an M.A. from the Johns Hopkins University, Paul H. Nitze School of Advanced International Studies (SAIS) and an A.B. from Hamilton College.

Shri Ranjit Singh Kalha, IFS (Retd)

Appointed to the Indian Foreign Service in 1965 and served in Indian Embassies at Hong Kong, Beijing and Tokyo. He has been Financial Advisor for Western Europe/Minister at High Commission, UK [London], Ambassador to Indonesia/ASEAN headquarters, Jakarta, Ambassador to Iraq, Joint Secretary Americas, USA & East Asia, China/Japan, Additional Secretary and Permanent Secretary, Ministry of External Affairs [1998-2002].

He has done extensive work pertaining to Political/Economic/Cultural Affairs with China, Japan, Koreas [ROK/DPRK], Mongolia, ASEAN States, Australia/New Zealand and Pacific Ocean States. He led India for the 6th, 7th and 8th Round of Boundary Talks with China, was a delegate, Paris Peace Talks/Cambodia [1989] and India's Representative/Commonwealth Secretariat [1980-84]. He represented India at G-15 Meetings, Jakarta 2001. He was involved in preparation of pamphlets 'Know your rights' series in all Indian languages and worked closely with International Human Rights Organisations, Human Rights Council, NGOs, Asia-Pacific Forum and implementation of International Treaty obligations by Government of India. He was appointed Member, National Human Rights Commission [2003-2008].

He has authored a book on Iraq entitled, *'The Ultimate Prize-Saddam and Oil'* published by Allied Publishers [2008] and has contributed articles to National Dailies. He regularly appears on TV and Radio broadcasts as commentator on National and International Events.

Professor Swaran Singh

Professor Swaran Singh is Chairman, Centre for International Politics, Organisation and Disarmament (CIPOD), School of International Studies (SIS), Jawaharlal Nehru University (New Delhi). He is also President of Association of Asia Scholars and General Secretary of Indian Association of Asian & Pacific Studies and Mentor at Centre for Conflict Resolution & Human Security (New Delhi).

Professor Singh is visiting Professor, University of Peace (Costa Rica) and Lady Sri Ram College (New Delhi). He is a former visiting Faculty of the Beijing University, Fudan University, Xiamen University, Shanghai Institute of International Studies.

Professor Singh is on the Editorial Board of *Asian Policy & Politics* (Washington DC), *Journal of the Indian Ocean Region* (Hyderabad), *Journal of Indian Ocean Studies* (Delhi), *and Millennial Asia* (Delhi), *Suraksha Chintan* (Meerut) as also Referee on various academic journals.

Professor Singh has travelled and written extensively on Asian Affairs, China's foreign and security policy issues with special focus on China-India confidence building measures as also on Arms Control and Disarmament, Peace and Conflict Resolution, India's foreign and security policy issues.

Dr Changsu Kim

Dr Changsu Kim is a senior research fellow at the Korea Institute for Defence Analyses (KIDA), a defence think tank affiliated with the ROK Ministry of National Defence in Seoul. He joined the Institute in 1985. Dr. Kim has served as Chief of Japan Studies Division, Chief of Regional Military Affairs Division, Chief of US Studies Division, Chief of International Conflict Studies Division and Director of the Centre for Security and Strategy. In 2007, he served as Special Assistant to the Minister for Policy at the ROK

Ministry of National Defence. From December 2008 to March 2009, he was a NIDS Fellow at the National Institute for Defence Studies, Tokyo, Japan. He is a member of the Planning and Coordination Committee of the National Unification Advisory Council, a constitutional organisation advising the ROK President on unification policy.

He is the principal writer of numerous KIDA reports, such as *The Changing US Military Deployment Strategy for the Asia-Pacific* (2011), *The Prospects for US-China Relations and South Korea's Strategic Responses* (2010), and *Non-military, Transnational Threats: Trends and Responses* (2007). His English books include *A New Alliance for the Next Century* (RAND, 1995), *Trilateral Naval Cooperation: Japan, US, Korea*.

He graduated from the Hankuk University of Foreign Studies in Seoul in 1977 and received his MA and Ph.D in Political Science from the University of Cincinnati in 1981 and 1985, respectively.

Shri Ranjan Mathai, Foreign Secretary

Born on May 24, 1952, Shri Mathai joined the Indian Foreign Service in 1974, after completing Post Graduate studies in Political Science at the University of Poona.

He has served in Indian Missions in Vienna, Colombo, Washington, Tehran and Brussels. As Joint Secretary (BSM) in the Ministry of External Affairs in New Delhi (January 1995 to February 1998), he headed the Division dealing with India's relations with Bangladesh, Sri Lanka, Myanmar and Maldives.

He was the Ambassador of India to Israel from February 1998 to June 2001 and to Qatar from August 2001 to July 2005. He held the post of Deputy High Commissioner of India to the UK in London, from August 2005 to January 2007. He served as the Ambassador of India to France with concurrent accreditation to the Principality of Monaco. Shri Mathai assumed the office of Foreign Secretary on 1 August 2011.

Major General GG Dwivedi, SM,VSM & BAR (Retd)

Major General GG Dwivedi, retired from the Army in 2009, after 38 years of distinguished service in the Infantry. He began his career as Platoon Commander in Bangladesh War, 1971. Later he commanded a battalion in Siachen, Mountain brigade in Kashmir Valley, a division in Manipur and South Assam, amidst intense Counter Insurgency environment and was decorated in command assignments.

A graduate from National Defence Academy and alumni of National Defence College, he has vast instructional and staff experience, including that of instructor at Indian Military Academy, Dehradun, Defence Services Staff College, Wellington and Defence attaché in China.

A keen student of strategy and international relations, he has an M Phil and a PhD degree. He is a visiting faculty at a number of defence/civil institutions.

His services were sought during the crucial stage of the Common Wealth Games (CWG) 2010 wherein he made valuable contribution in the successful conduct of the event. Currently he is involved in Youth Empowerment Initiatives. He writes regularly for various professional journals and national dailies.

Vice Admiral Hideaki Kaneda, JMSDF (Retd)

Vice Admiral Hideaki Kaneda is Director of The Okazaki Institute, an adjunct fellow of JIIA (Japan Institute of International Affairs) and a trustee of RIPS (Research Institute of Peace and Security). He has worked as Senior Fellow of Asia Centre and a Guest Professor of Faculty of Policy Management of Keio University.

He has authorised a number of books and articles pertaining to security issues, including "Proposal for Maritime Coalition in East Asia", IMDEX, Germany, November 2000, "Changing situation of China's and Japan's security", World and Japan, Tokyo, September 2001, "US/China Power Game in Maritime Hegemony", JIIA, Tokyo, March 2003, "BMD for Japan", Kaya-Books, Tokyo, March 2003, "Multilateral Multi-Agencies Cooperation for Maritime Order Maintenance", CSCAP, Apr. 2005, "US and Japan's Policy toward North Korea", World and Japan, Tokyo, Sep. 2005, "Japan's Missile Defence", JIIA, Tokyo, Dec. 2006, "Collective Defence Right and Japan's Security", Naigai News, Tokyo, Aug. 2007, "Aspects of the War (Sea Battle)", Naigai Publishing Company, Tokyo, July. 2008, "Understanding BMD", Ikaros-Books, Tokyo, Oct. 2008.

He is a graduate of the National Defence Academy, the Maritime War College and the US Naval War College. He served in the JMSDF from 1968 to 1999, primarily in Naval Surface Warfare at sea, and in Naval and Joint Plans and Policy Making on shore.

Dr James E. Auer

Dr James E. Auer is Director of the Centre for US-Japan Studies and Cooperation at the Vanderbilt Institute for Public Policy Studies. The US-Japan Centre hosts a half dozen or more Japanese researchers annually on the Vanderbilt campus. Dr. Auer teaches US-Japan relations and the history of sea power to Vanderbilt University graduate and undergraduate students. He served in the US Navy from 1963 to 1983 in a number of assignments, largely in Japan. These included visiting student at the Japan Maritime Self-Defence Force Staff College in Tokyo and commanding officer of a guided missile frigate homeported in Yokosuka. From April 1979 until September 1988, he served as Special Assistant for Japan in the Office of the Secretary of Defence. He holds an A.B. degree from Marquette University and a Ph.D from the Fletcher School of Law and Diplomacy, Tufts University. His thesis, *The Postwar Rearmament of Japanese Maritime Forces 1945-1971*, was published in English by Praeger Publishers and in Japanese translation by the Jiji Press under the title *Yomigaeru Nippon Kaigun*. In December 2009, he received the Japanese Government's "Order of Rising Sun, Gold Rays with Neck Ribbon" award presented by Consul General of Japan, Nashville, TN on behalf of the Emperor of Japan.

Lieutenant General Takayoshi Ogawa (Retd)

Japan Air Self-Defence Force (JASDF) Lieutenant General Takayoshi OGAWA (Retd) graduated from the National Defence Academy in 1973.

He was assigned an Aircraft Control and Warning Group as a Weapon Controller. After graduating from the Air Command and Staff College, USAF, USA, he held several assignments in Air Staff Office and Operation Wings. In 1993, he graduated from National Institute for Defence Studies, Japan and attened National War College, Washington D.C. USA in 1995. He holds a Master's degree in National Strategy of Security Studies. In 1999, he assumed the position of Commander, Western Aircraft Control and Warning Wing, JASDF. In 2003, he became the Vice Commander, Air Support Command, JASDF. In 2006, he took over as the Commander, Air Development and Test Command, JASDF.

Since his retirement in 2007, he is serving as a General Advisor, in Electronic Products and Systems Group, Mitsubishi Electric Company in Tokyo and is a Special Research Fellow at the Okazaki Institute for studying international security strategies.

Lieutenant General Masahiro Kunimi (Retd)

Lieutenant General Masahiro Kunimi is the Director, Institute For World Politics and Economy in Tokyo, Japan. Prior to joining the Institute, he was the Director General of Cabinet Satellite Intelligence Centre, Cabinet Office from April 2001 to Mar 2005. Lt Gen Kunimi served as the Director General of The Defence Intelligence Headquarters (JDIH), Ministry of Defence from Jan 1997 to Dec 1999.

He also served as the Defence Attaché, Japan Embassy in People's Republic of China (PRC) from May 1983 to Jun 1986. He graduated from the Intelligence school, DIA, DOD,USA, the National Institute for Defence Studies, Japan and Staff College JGSDF.

Other Participants

1. Lieutenant General Bang Hyo-Bok (KIDA, RoK)
2. Sr Col Tran Hua Hung (IDIR, Vietnam)
3. Dr Shao Yuqun (SIIS, China)

ACRONYMS

S.NO.	SHORT FORM	FULL FORM
1	AAR	Anti Aircraft Artillery
2	ADMM+	ASEAN Defence Ministers' Meeting – Plus comprises – US, India, Australia, Russia and New Zealand and ASEAN – plus three
3	AFTA	ASEAN Free Trade Area
4	APEC	Asia Pacific Economic Co-operation
5	ARF	ASEAN Regional Forum
6	ASAT	Anti Satellite
7	ASEAN	Association of South East Asian Nations
8	ASEAN-plus-three	ASEAN, China, Japan, South Korea
9	ASTEP	Astrobiology Science and Technology for Exploring Planets
10	BRIC	Brazil, India and China
11	BRICS	Brazil, India, China, South Africa
12	CELT	Centres of English Language Training
13	CEPA	Comprehensive Economic Cooperation Agreement
14	CIVITS	China, India, Vietnam, Indonesia, Turkey and South Africa
15	CVID	Complete, Verifiable and Irreversible Dismantlement
16	DOC	Declaration on Conduct
17	EAS	East Asia Summit
18	ECFA	Economic Co-operation Framework Agreement
19	EDC	Entrepreneurship Development Centres
20	EU	European Union
21	EVSL	Early Voluntary Sectoral Liberalisation

22	FTA	Free Trade Area
23	FTAAP	Free Trade Area of the Asia Pacific
24	ITC	Information Telecommunication and Computing
25	JMSFD	Japanese Maritime Self Defence Force
26	NATO	North Atlantic Treaty Organisation
27	NEACD	North East Asia Cooperation Dialogue
28	NFU	No First Use
29	NWS	Nuclear Weapon States
30	OAA	Open Agent Architecture
31	OECD	Organisation for Economic Cooperation and Development
32	PSI	Proliferation Security Initiative
33	TAC	Treaty of Amity and Co-operation
34	TAR	Tibet Autonomous Region
35	TPP	Trans-Pacific Partnership
36	TSD	Trilateral Strategic Dialogue (comprises the US, Japan and Australia)
37	UNCLOS	UN Convention on the Law of the Sea
38	UNSC	United Nations Security Council
39	WMD	Weapons of Mass Destruction

INAUGURAL SESSION

Welcome Address   —   Vice Admiral Shekhar Sinha, AVSM, NM & Bar, CISC and President, USI Council.

Keynote Address   —   Admiral Nirmal Verma, PVSM, AVSM, ADC, Chairman, COSC and Chief of the Naval Staff.

Special Addresses   —   Lieutenant General Tran Thai Binh, IDS, Vietnam.

  —   Lieutenant General Bang, Hyo-Bok (Retd), KIDA, RoK.

Concluding Remarks   —   Lieutenant General PK Singh, PVSM, AVSM (Retd), Director, USI.

WELCOME ADDRESS

Vice Admiral Shekhar Sinha, AVSM, NM & Bar
CISC and President, USI Council

21st Century has witnessed the emergence of the Asia-Pacific region as a key driver of global politics. Stretching from the Indian subcontinent to the western shores of America, the region includes countries from South, SE, East and NE Asia, together with countries of the Pacific Rim. The region spans the Pacific Ocean and the Indian Ocean, which are inextricably linked to maritime trade, geo-strategic equations and geo-political calculus. It boasts of a population of around 4 bn, out of the world's population of 7 bn and includes many of the emerging key engines of the global economy like China, India, ROK and Indonesia. While Europe and USA are confronting economic stagnation and recession, this region has registered an enviable growth rate of over 7 per cent and accounts for more than 60 per cent of the world's GDP. By 2020, seven of the world's largest economies will be from this region.

The Asia-Pacific region embodies a growing web of complex interdependence and shared interests that can provide the foundation and impetus for cooperative engagement. There are significant stakes in preserving the security and freedom of the sea lanes which are vital to the economic growth. Other areas of common interest include Counter-terrorism, Counter-proliferation, Humanitarian assistance and disaster relief and possibly many more.

I would say that the region is also facing a number of security challenges such as Korean peninsula, across the Taiwan Strait, in the East China Sea and more importantly, in the South China Sea. There are some other issues of lesser magnitude like the ownership of the Kurile Islands and that of

Dokdo and Takeshima Islands.

China's growing power and assertiveness, doubts over sustained regional US presence and dominance in the future, escalating anxiety over North Korea's nuclear and missile programs and renewed worries about Taiwan's security have triggered a marked increase in defence spending. Peaceful resolution of these disputes will be vital for the continued economic growth and well being of people in the region. This would require carefully structured and adequately empowered security architecture.

Prior to the 1990s, very few channels for regional security dialogue existed in the Asia-Pacific. Regional groupings like the South East Asia Treaty Organisation and the Asian and Pacific Council were established in the sixties, but collapsed by mid seventies. With its genesis from this legacy, was born the more successful sub-regional grouping, the Association of South East Asian Nations or ASEAN. Founded in 1967, ASEAN expanded via several avenues, including a major security component called the ASEAN Regional Forum. It was best suited to provide the basis for this architecture, but even ASEAN's initial collaborative functions were essentially economic, political and cultural. As a consequence, bilateral, US-led cooperation tended to be the primary mode of Asia-Pacific security collaboration throughout the Cold War period.

The US is, without any doubt, the dominant power in the Pacific, with enduring engagement in the Asia-Pacific Region. Its military power is centred around the US Pacific Command, the biggest of the unified combatant commands of the US Armed Forces, responsible for the defence of the Mariannas islands and the Federated States of Micronesia.

Moving westwards to Asia, the US has five major allies in Japan, ROK, Philippines, Taiwan and Australia. With Japan, the US has the treaty of 1960, which provides for stationing of US troops in Japan and authorises intervention by the US, for the defence of Japan and its island territories. This has led to incremental creation of 135 bases in Japan and stationing of over 52,000 troops, including 15,000 marines.

With ROK, USA has the mutual defence treaty of 1953, providing US defence umbrella to South Korea against external threats, including nuclear threats. The US presently has a strength of 28,500 troops in ROK, with the eighth US Army and the seventh US Air Force stationed in 70 bases.

The US-Taiwan relations date back to 1954. The Taiwan Relations Act 1979 requires US to sell defence equipment to Taiwan, as necessary, for Taiwan to maintain its self defence capability, but the US is not bound to get involved in any conflict for defence of Taiwan.

Under the US-Philippines military base agreement of 1947, US had secured a 99 year lease for 16 bases, which included the Subic Bay and the Clark Air Base. However, US Forces withdrew from Philippines in Nov 1992, consequent to large scale public resentment to the stationing of US troops. This heralded the somewhat decline in the US maritime power in the Asia-Pacific. Quick to sense the void, China claimed Mischief Reef in the Spratly group of islands, within the EEZ of Philippines, in 1994.

America's Asia-Pacific alliances remain an integral component of the region's security architecture and notwithstanding the process of 'transformation' which this system of alliances is undergoing to accommodate the dynamics of the post 9/11 strategic environment, some of these relationships (namely the US–Japan and US–Australia alliances) have actually strengthened during the period since the end of the Cold War, contrary to the expectations of conventional theories of alliance politics. New mechanisms such as the US–Japan–South Korea Trilateral Coordination and Oversight Group and the US–Japan–Australia Trilateral Strategic Dialogue have been formed to address emerging security issues at both the regional and global levels. This 'expansive bilateralism' has been supplemented since the early 1990s by a steady growth in regional institutions, arrangements and structures. According to one recent estimate, over 100 such channels now exist at the official (Track 1) level, including such leading regional security institutions as the ASEAN Regional Forum, the Shanghai Cooperation Organisation and the East Asia Summit, which, despite their largely economic focus, still have the potential to emerge as potent East Asian security mechanisms.

There are ad hoc or issue-specific treaties or regimes like the North Korean Six Party Talks (6PT) or Proliferation Security Initiative (PSI), aimed at combating Weapons of Mass Destruction (WMD) trafficking. It is significant that these components of the extant regional security architecture all display immense structural variation in their purpose, membership, formalisation, scope and capabilities. For example, Asia Pacific Economic Cooperation is pan-regional in its membership, but confined to economic, rather than security governance at present, while the US-alliance system is indisputably powerful in its defence capabilities, but exclusive in its membership. The growth in institutions and dialogues at the unofficial (or Track 2) level has been even more profound, with over 200 such channels now estimated to be in existence.

The moot point, however, is what is the relative role and efficacy of the existing instruments of security governance which I have just enumerated. There is general, but not universal consensus that ASEAN and its various offshoots (ASEAN+3, ASEAN Regional Forum) act as the linchpin for 'community building' in the Asia-Pacific region. The development of the East Asia Summit (EAS) around this fulcrum certainly offers promising potential, though many argue that the incorporation of the US into the EAS would be imperative for its success. APEC has the benefit of being a genuinely pan-regional organisation, but does not enjoy a good track record in security governance or even economic governance for that matter. The SCO is a relative newcomer and though regarded as effective within its limited domain, does not appeal widely to the remainder of the region.

In addition to developing current institutions, there have been proposals for new initiatives. Foremost among these has been Australia's call for an 'Asia-Pacific Community' (APC). This envisages a new truly pan-regional institution (specifically including India, plus the US), which will be able to engage in the full spectrum of dialogue, cooperation and action on economic and political matters and future challenges related to security. Unfortunately, this initiative seems to have gained little traction beyond its rhetorical stage.

The appetite for new institutions is weak, especially when they have to compete with other political projects such as the EAS and offers no tangible value-addition at this stage. Other new alternatives such as a Northeast Asia Security Forum, based upon the 6 Party Talks, or a Sino-American 'G2', have even dimmer prospects at this time. Hence, the future will most likely involve working to improve upon what institutions and associations we already have, to achieve a stable regional security regime.

A preliminary assessment reveals that China stands out as the primary concern in the region. This is notwithstanding the fact that its market with the ASEAN states, touches a whopping 300 bn US$ and that its booming economy has infact propelled the growth of the regional economies. China's meteoric rise, therefore, merits a careful study.

In the last fifteen years, China has emerged as a global economic and military power. With a GDP touching 5 trillion dollars and foreign exchange reserves crossing the 2.4 trillion dollars mark, a cash-flushed China embarked on a well orchestrated strategy to enhance its influence in the Asia-Pacific region.

Economic and Security Architecture in the Asia-Pacific

The question of a suitable regional security architecture for the Asia-Pacific region has been raised during various seminars and conferences. The key contours of the debate involve the nature of 'security architecture', the effectiveness of its existing components and the prospects for developing a mature and stable regional order in the future. This seminar is also one such initiative to deliberate on this vital issue.

So far the security arrangements established by the USA, in the Asia-Pacific region have been bilateral. It is now attempting to build up trilateral security groupings like USA, Australia and Japan, USA, India and Japan and even USA and India with ROK or Australia.

The ASEAN, in contrast, is a multilateral association. I am sure the seminar will study the advantages of multilateral groupings in terms of the collective security they provide and the pressure they can bring to bear on a target country. In this context, multilateral forums involving extra-regional states, such as the ASEAN Defence Ministers Meeting Plus and the East

Asia Summit, have shown considerable promise and potency.

In my view, the security architecture for the Asia-Pacific Region must be open and inclusive, allowing stakeholders, big or small, to "plug in and play", to have the opportunity to have their "voice" heard and to work together to resolve issues of concern.

It should be inclusive and extensive, from the Indian Peninsula to the Pacific, including the entire Eurasian landmass and the Pacific Rim. It should be plural or multilateral and its institutions should be consultative, respecting consensual solutions.

I am sure that this seminar will focus on these issues and more and that the deliberations will throw up tangible solutions which can help structure an inclusive and broad based and an adequately empowered and effective security architecture for the Asia Pacific Region. I would like to compliment the USI for bringing together a galaxy of domain experts to offer their views. I wish the Seminar every success.

KEYNOTE ADDRESS

Admiral Nirmal Verma, PVSM, AVSM, ADC
Chairman, COSC and Chief of the Naval Staff

The global significance of the Asia-Pacific region is universally recognised. In some quarters, the times that we live in are referred to as – the "Asia-Pacific Century". India undertook a strategic shift, when in 1991, we first enunciated our 'Look East' policy. This policy has since matured beyond its genesis, as an economic instrument into what is today our strategic vision of the evolving global order and our role in the comity of nations. Speaking about our 'Look East Policy', our Prime Minister, Dr Manmohan Singh has said and I quote *'most of all it is about reaching out to our civilizational neighbours'*. This is a view that has, in fact, been supported and encouraged by many others. In her last visit to India, in July 2011, US Secretary of State Hillary Clinton endorsed India's role in the future of the Asia-Pacific, in the 21st Century.

Being naturally interested in matters military and maritime, two aspects particularly strike me as I reflect upon the region. The first is that the region has a distinct maritime footprint, not only because the dispersed Asia-Pacific nations are linked via the oceans, but also because the sea is a lifeline for economic growth in the region. The Asia Pacific is home to numerous major shipping lanes which service regional as well as global trade. Disruption of traffic flow on these routes could thus have a severe impact on the global economy. The second aspect relates to defence spending. The statistics are staggering by any account. In 2010, the Asia Pacific accounted for more than 63 per cent of global defence spending. Even excluding the US from these figures, because their defence budget exceeds many a national budget, the countries of the region accounted for more than 35 per cent of the non-US-global defence spending, with rising trends.

These trends of defence expenditure require to be viewed in the backdrop of the agreements for cooperative engagements that have existed between nations, in the region, over the past half century or so. Some groupings, such as the OIC and OPEC, include parts of, but also reach beyond the region. Others are groupings, such as the APEC, the SAARC, the Shanghai Cooperation Organisation that include some, but not all countries of the region. Yet others are agreements and alliances, such as the CSTO, the ANZUS, the Five Power Defence Arrangement, as well as bilateral treaties and agreements, involving the USA. Besides these, the region has other sets of nations with strong military links even though formal treaties are not enunciated. Such agreements may have long served the requirements as they existed, but it may now be a necessity to review these commitments in the context of newer and future challenges. These challenges vary from economic matters to security issues such as territorial disputes, terrorism, nuclear proliferation by state as well as non state actors, energy security, piracy, Humanitarian Assistance and disaster relief and climate change.

The economic factor garners renewed attention as the economic landscape of the Asia-Pacific is rapidly changing with the rise of Asia as the global economic powerhouse. The Asia-Pacific region today accounts for over half of the world's population and contributes a third of the global GDP in Purchasing Power Parity terms. Asia itself is expected to gain further prominence since it is expected to account for almost 45 per cent of the word's GDP, 1/3rd of global trade and 25 per cent of the military expenditure by 2020. This remarkable growth has nevertheless created a variety of security challenges for the region, which merit our attention. As the inhabitants of the Asia- Pacific region, as we move up the growth trajectory, it would be in the global interest to ensure a cooperative economic and peaceful security environment that spurs growth and prosperity for the entire region.

Diversity is the hallmark of this region. The Asia-Pacific region is economically and politically diverse. It contains some of the world's largest and most vibrant economies and some of its smallest and most fragile States. The Asia-Pacific region is the most 'disaster prone' area in the world, with nearly half of all natural disasters occurring in this area. Many people in the region live on flood plains and in coastal areas exposed to cyclones, Tsunamis and other such natural calamities. Such adversity requires the countries of the region to come together and build cooperative capacities to overcome the vagaries of nature.

On the brighter side, by 2020, seven of the world's ten leading economies are likely to be in the Asia-Pacific region. During the economic meltdown in 2008, this region remained the fastest growing economy, globally. China and India, growing at 9.5 and 8.5 per cent respectively, are two of the fastest growing economies in this region. With the severe downturn of the economies in Europe, it is but natural that this region holds the global attention to reinvigorate the momentum in other regions as well. The fact that the current economic crisis in Europe is perhaps the first in which intervention by Asian economies is eagerly solicited, indicates the strength of Asia - Pacific region; as does the increasing role of Asia, especially China and India as consumers of resources and their influence in international economic relations.

Politically, the Asia - Pacific region would register all forms of Governments varying from Democracies to Kingdoms to Dictatorships. This, according to many, has been an impediment in political and economic engagement amongst the states in the region. Mechanisms have to be devised to bridge these differences of perception.

We are seeing a certain edginess in the relations between the countries of this region. The potential for conflict in the South China Sea and the instability of the Korean Peninsula have heightened the awareness of policymakers, scholars and analysts to the region's shortcomings, in terms of institutional arrangements, to resolve potential crises. The South China Sea, in particular, is an area of significant concern. The leaders of the world's two most successful surviving communist parties met in Beijing last month. Chairman of Chinese Communist Party hosted his Vietnamese counterpart for official talks, with the two sides agreeing to work together to solve their territorial dispute in the South China Sea. The developments in the South China Sea and the outcomes will have major implications, not only for the countries in the region, but for the world at large, as many nations have considerable economic interests in the region.

With that as the backdrop, it is appropriate that we brain storm on the structure and content of the security architecture that would offer a 'best fit' to promote peace and stability, owing to the peculiarities of the region. Precisely for this reason, readymade solutions do not exist and it may not also be feasible to borrow an existing arrangement functioning in another region to be applied in the Asia – Pacific.

A scan of the multitude of threats that exist makes it apparent that unilateralism, as a strategy, may be inadequate and that multilateral cooperative mechanisms are the way forward. Therefore, there exists a compelling need to assess the threats faced and the opportunities that exist to leverage for ensuring peace and stability in the region. As most would agree, many contemporary issues that impinge upon the peace and stability of the region are beyond the capacity of any one country to handle single-handedly and, therefore, require cooperative and collective action. The ongoing deliberations regarding multilateral effort under the aegis of the United Nations, in combating piracy, could also be a model used to deliberate if it can be applied in the region.

On piracy, as we all are aware, there is more to fighting it than just military action. To quote the UN Secretary General "Piracy is not a waterborne disease." It, indeed, is a spill over of governance deficit, myriad socio-economic issues and lawlessness for which a collective initiative seems to be the only way forward. In order to tackle all these issues, global level responses may be optimal, but problems which are primarily regional in scope and character are best dealt with at a regional level, considering the limitations of time, commitment of attention and resources at the global level. A multilateral engagement, comprising a holistic representation of the stakeholder nations is the desired way ahead. In the same breath, I would emphasise that some nations may deem bilateralism, trilateralism, or even an informal arrangement as more appropriate to a particular situation and, therefore, such perspectives should not be misunderstood. These arrangements may in fact be most appropriate in a particular context as has been adequately demonstrated by the success of ReCAAP. Enhanced engagements with holistic inclusion of all stakeholder nations must be the guiding principle or – *'mantra'* as we call it in India.

What makes the process hard is that Asia–Pacific includes states which experience deep political differences in their relations. Significant economic and religious differences amongst the states are also a reality. Hence, according to me, addressing the underlying security issues must begin with Confidence Building Measures. Drawing from the Conference on Interaction and Confidence Building Measures in Asia, we could develop CBMs across economic, environmental, human and military-political dimensions for countering new challenges and threats. I would, therefore, like to state that mechanisms for cooperative engagement at different levels should be encouraged, in the spirit of seeking common ground while reserving differences. Inspiring leadership and statesmanship play crucial role in resolving differences and ensuring peace and stability in the world. In my opinion, the Asia- Pacific is no different.

The requirement of an effective security architecture is essential because, Asia's economic growth and its population size, its productive capacity and its demand, its technological leadership and the geopolitical importance of its major actors are all contributing to the shift of the global centre of gravity towards Asia. There are profound changes taking place in the Asia-Pacific, which have influenced global affairs and are likely to do so in the near future. In the coming years, the region will be able to exert greater influence over global politics, shifting the fulcrum of political power too, towards it.

In light of the myriad of challenges that exist in the region, there is the requirement of a comprehensive mechanism or mechanisms, which are inclusive, efficient and adequately representative. This would unleash the real potential of the countries in the region towards growth and prosperity. The question that this seminar seeks is - What is the kind of security architecture that would suit the region?

Though I have talked about enhanced engagements with holistic inclusion utilising both multilateral and bilateral approaches, at the regional and sub – regional levels, I am sure that, given the collective wisdom, experience and diversity amongst the delegates of this seminar, we would be experiencing enormous choice in terms of proposals that would be put forward. I must also share my belief that gatherings such as these, provide valuable insights which influence policy and international action, taking us one step closer to a potential solution to persisting challenges.

I, once again, thank the Director, USI for allowing me the opportunity to share my thoughts on such a topical issue. I wish the delegates all the very best and hope the seminar is successful in debating and evaluating the many possibilities that lie before the Asia - Pacific.

SPECIAL ADDRESS

Lieutenant General Tran Thai Binh, PhD, Vietnam People's Army (VPA)

In recent years, security situations in the region as well as in the world have changed profoundly, unpredictably and complicatedly. Although peace and stability remain the major trend, there are some factors which may bring the risk of instability of the security situation in the Asia-Pacific. These are: territorial disputes, arms race, threat to use force and use of force in international relations, national, ethnic, religious conflicts and non-traditional security threats.

I would like to focus on two issues. The first one is territorial disputes. These continue to be increasingly complicated. The second is the threat of the use of force in international relations; the intervention into other countries' internal affairs tend to be more serious. For outstanding issues between two countries, or among countries, we need to make honest efforts and participation of the international community.

The international community cannot act as bystanders. They have to shoulder responsibility, enhance cooperation, settle issues on the basis of international laws, move together to seek solutions for dispute and enhance and maintain peace, stability and development. In particular, the United States, Russia, China and India should play more of a role in regional issues. The relations between or among major powers have an important role in international relations. Major Powers in the region should be more responsible and set good examples in implementing international laws.

The organisation of this conference by the USI is an essential and productive activity to enhance security in the region. It is also a manifestation of the will to shoulder more responsibility by India as a major power in the region. In my opinion, the Seminar is a good opportunity for think tanks to exchange information, consolidate mutual understanding and build confidence among countries in the region. It is also a good opportunity for think tanks and institutions to enhance cooperation in the academic field; learn from each other in order to seek productive solutions and help in maintaining peace and stability in the region.

I am confident that the Seminar will be successful. As a follow up, there will be other meetings to discuss and find out solutions to enhance cooperation and make Asia Pacific a peaceful and prosperous region.

SPECIAL ADDRESS

Lieutenant General Bang Hyo-Bok (Retd) President, Korea Institute for Defence Analyses (KIDA)

I don't think anyone is opposed to the idea of peace and security in the region. We face a lot of obstacles though. The world is getting smaller everyday. Each country has its own problems, all related in terms of how they impact others. Different countries employ different means to solve them. Some countries use terrorism, some like to talk of using nuclear weapons or chemical weapons. I still believe that we are here today to resolve some of these threats spoken about. South Korea has its own unique domestic problems. All countries whose representatives are present here this morning have their own problems, though there is some commonality between them.

There is no more acceptance of the use of force, nuclear power or any means that go against human nature. We have got to be more open minded about the problems we are facing and regarding the knowledge and wisdom of others. The need to respect differences in cultures and ideas is also urgent. I would like to encourage everyone to gather wisdom and ideas from all the discussions in the sessions. If anyone wants to explore more security issues with South Korea, they can feel free to contact me during the Seminar and ask me for data or information.

I conclude my speech by introducing some of the facts and data of my institution to you. Lt General PK Singh visited my institution in late April 2011. My institution is under the Ministry of National Defence. We are a military think-tank and I have some 430 staff members. We have centres like those of security strategy, military acquisition and military strategy. If you have a chance to visit South Korea, do come to my institution. I will be available for meaningful interaction and fruitful discussions.

CONCLUDING REMARKS

Lieutenant General PK Singh, PVSM, AVSM (Retd)
Director, USI

The theme of the seminar is Peace and Stability in the Asia-Pacific Region: Assessment of the Security Architecture. I will not wrap up what happened in the three sessions, except to highlight the point, that irrespective of what happens, there will always be national interests, there will be regional and global interests, there will be bilateral and multilateral relations, there will be different subjects thrown up and we have discussed a number of them, including a subject like rare earths.

In our endeavour, we are looking at the difference between what happened with the APEC and its emergence. It started with non controversial matters like non-traditional threats etc. It is only of late that it is bringing on the table, traditional threats, like maritime security and proliferation. The time taken by them to come to this point is reflective of some of the challenges of evolving regional architectures. I was reading an article about the EAS this morning, describing the evolution of ASEAN to the EAS, which raised the question of whether the mechanism has been effective. Even in the seminar, concerns were raised about such platforms being talk shops and some rightly pointed out that even if that were the case, there was intrinsic merit in talking and that is an important facet of diplomacy.

The article posed the question that, in the absence of these organisations, would there have been regional conflict and less effective ways to respond to such challenges? I think it is very important to consider the counter scenario while assessing the efficacy of regional mechanisms. I think credit should be given where it is due and in the final analysis, such existing mechanisms have brought us together here today.

My personal belief is that we are now evolving an architecture without having fought a war, without peace being forced on anybody, thus one which promises to be more practical and more acceptable to everyone. With our wisdom, I hope we find answers to all difficult things.

SESSION I

STRATEGIC AND SECURITY ENVIRONMENT IN THE ASIA PACIFIC REGION

Auditorium

Chairman	-	Shri SK Bhutani, IFS (Retd).
First Paper	-	Professor Zhao Gancheng, SIIS, China.
Second Paper	-	Mr Tetsuo Kotani, Okazaki Institute, Japan.
Third Paper	-	Dr Michael Pillsbury, DOD, USA.

Seminar Room 1

Chairman	-	Mr Fyodor Lukyanov, Editor-in-Chief, *Russia in Global Affairs*.
First Paper	-	Professor Bharat Karnad, CPR.
Second Paper	-	Sr. Col Tran Hau Hung, IDIR, Vietnam.
Third Paper	-	Ambassador Andrea Perugini, MOFA, Italy.

Discussion (In Auditorium)

SESSION I

STRATEGIC AND SECURITY ENVIRONMENT IN THE ASIA PACIFIC REGION

Session I (Auditorium)
Chairman's Opening Remarks

Shri SK Bhutani, IFS (Retd)

I do not have to introduce the speakers to you, as their bio data is given in the booklets. On my right, we have Prof Zhao Gancheng, who is a senior fellow and director of South Asia Studies at the Shanghai Institute of International Studies. He will present to us the Chinese perspective on nuclear issues in the region. To my left is Mr Kotani, a special fellow at the Okazaki Institute at Tokyo. He specialises in US-Japan relations. Dr Pillsbury is no stranger to India. He is an alumni from Stanford and Colombia and has worked later in close collaboration with the Kennedy government. He is also the author of the proposal to establish intelligence and military ties with China, pursued subsequently by the Regan administration.

I was very impressed by the inaugural speeches and the theme implicit in them, that of inclusiveness. We are looking today not at confrontation but an inclusive architecture for security in the Asia-Pacific region. The world today is strewn with divisive issues, be it the economic crises of the West, or the uncertain promise of the Arab spring closer home. With the West thus mired in uncertainty, East Asia and Indian Ocean area should look to lend stability to a turbulent world.

I look forward to such an approach in the papers to be presented as well as the questions that participants may ask. The effort should be to look for ways to build an inclusive, stable and progressive Asia-Pacific Region.

May I now invite Prof Zhao Gancheng from China to make his presentation.

Session I

First Paper (Auditorium)

Professor Zhao Gancheng (China)

Strategic and Security Environment in the Asia Pacific Region: A Chinese Perspective on Nuclear Issues

The Asia-Pacific region is the focus of development, not only for economic growth, but also for security development with a variety of trends. One of them is the nuclear development, which is seen as quite explosive and potentially very risky. While the Asia-Pacific region has witnessed rapid development with growth in some of its developing powers like China, India and others, both the historic remains left over from the Cold War and newly developing trends are presenting a number of security issues, leading to uncertainties. The North Korea nuclear issue and Iran nuclear development might be two representatives as far as security environment in Asia is concerned. Besides, the Asia-Pacific region as a whole has concentration of nuclear weapons states (NWS), including the existing and potential ones. The regional nuclear situation tends to cause concerns in both the NWS and non-NWS. For instance, China itself is an NWS and is surrounded by other NWS. From the Chinese perspective, it is hard to regard it as a positive development. Similar is the case with other NWS. Understanding the implication of the situation requires a broad view on the international development in general and a new look at causes that might have led to the situation in specific countries.

The background of international development

The end of the Cold War brought about a new structure of the international system. Instead of the rivalry of the two ideologically confrontational blocs, the United States began to play a decisive role in determining the general trend and direction of the system. What was known as the sole superpower system should have produced quite different dynamics as far as nuclear deterrence was concerned. As deterrence stems from perception of threat, the post-Cold War arrangement made it possible for all the NWS to reassess threats. And that explains the reason the United States put non-proliferation as one of the foreign policy pillars. In other words, the NWS, led by the United States could have found some common grounds in this regard, that is, preventing all the other non-NWS from getting nuclear. That was based on a seemingly rational assumption that the NWS, by then, would no longer threaten each other with WMD and what the international society should have done was only to stop all the other non-NWS attempts to develop nuclear weapons. However, that logic did not work.

Firstly, the collapse of the Soviet Union did not eliminate threats. Despite the fact that the confrontation between the two blocs was gone, there were all other kinds of rivalries, conflicts and confrontations persistently existing. In the Asia-Pacific, the cold war legacy was present. Asia used to be the battle field during the Cold War and the simple fact was that the confrontational forces still saw the security environment in Asia as being as unsafe as it had been.

Secondly, the concept of threat changed. Threat to national security used to be seen as product of state, but the post-Cold War era witnessed the rise of non-state actors that played increasingly important roles in the security environment. The peak was, of course, the 9/11 terrorist attack. It is not clear if that situation made states less desirable to get nuclear weapons, but it is quite clear that non-state actors would like to get whatsoever they could in order to realise their goals. That led to more interactions in WMD fields.

Thirdly, the existing non-proliferation regime does not find itself justified in norms, ideas and policy practice, etc. and, therefore, difficult to make it acceptable to all the members of the international community. The reality, that some nations possess nuclear weapons legitimately and others cannot do so, set up a very annoying example in international relations. This is a *de facto* double standard, hardly justified in the real policy arena.

Last but not the least was that the US-dominated international system took the concerns of only some of its members seriously. In fact, the United States did not want to see some of them as members of the international community and were described by President Bush after 9/11 as the 'axis of evils'. The implications conveyed very negative messages to those countries like North Korea, Iran, Iraq, Myanmar etc.. It is not incidental that these countries want to develop nuclear weapons. It was in that context that the nuclear crises occurred. The Asia-Pacific region has to carry the biggest burden in this regard. There are potential conflicts in the region. As far as nuclear development is concerned, the region is expected to have more difficulties to deal with the nuclear issues in the near future.

After the 9/11 terror attack, the international environment has undergone even more dramatic changes. The United States shifted its strategic priorities, focussing on the international campaign against terror. The two American waged wars carried out massive strikes on extremist groups, but could not achieve goals set by the Bush administration. Instead, both the Afghan and Iraqi wars led to endless conflicts, resulting in heavy casualties. Meanwhile, the wars have affected neighbouring countries, resulting in more turbulence in the countries like Pakistan, some Central Asian states, etc. Again, nuclear issues have come up as a security concern on whether extremist groups might have opportunities to possess WMD, or whether nuclear weapons might fall into what are known as wrong hands.

The trends are far from satisfactory. The new world order has not yet taken real shape and nobody really knows whether the world needs a new order. The Asia-Pacific situation looks more complicated. There is no inclusive and comprehensive architecture for regional security, though we do have a number of sub-regional and multilateral institutions. However, when an acute issue such as a nuclear crisis comes up, the region will not have a mature mechanism to handle it. The failure of the Six-Party Talks has been one of the examples.

Now the United States is shifting its strategic priorities, arguably from anti-terror, to focus more on the Asia-Pacific region, in national interests. In this context, nuclear development in the region could come up again and challenge the existing security structures of the region. That would test the validity of the current non-proliferation regime.

The validity of non-proliferation regime in Asia-Pacific

The non-proliferation regime is one of the pillars of the international system. The validity of the regime including that of the NPT, CTBT and other treaties is extremely important for defending the integrity of the international system. However, the regime was born with an assumption that all the NWS which acquired nuclear weapons before the treaty could possess them and other nations should never try to get the weapons. Unfortunately, that assumption does not work very well simply because the regime based on the assumption neither demands the already existing NWS to eliminate what they have, nor take into account, concerns of the other countries that still feel threatened in one or the other way. In Asia, the two factors play the role in stimulating nuclear development in the region.

At the first level, the issue is whether the five legitimate NWS began to work towards final elimination of their WMD. Again, since the birth of the non-proliferation regime, there has been little progress in this regard, even though the collapse of the Soviet Union created relatively favourable conditions. Compared to the Cold War period, during the past two decades achievement should have been more. But the reality is not so. It is not because the five NWS see each other as hostile and need to keep the stockpile to deter. Rather, it is because they want to keep monopoly in this area and the United States in particular which possesses both the largest nuclear stockpile and most advanced conventional weapon systems. Even if the most militarily powerful country wants to keep sufficient deterrence against others, how can it demand that all other members of the international community should follow the non-proliferation regime faithfully? In other words, as long as nuclear weapons are seen as useful deterrence means, the non-proliferation regime in the contemporary context is hardly expected to succeed.

At the second level, the issue is not whether countries still feel threatened; the real issue is why some countries still believe that the nuclear weapon is a rational option when they feel threatened? As nuclear weapons are not usable weapons in a civilized world, any determination to develop nuclear weapons has to contain a number of elements. From a cost-benefit view-point, possessing nuclear weapons is certainly a substantial symbol for a nation's military capability, which can be used to deter other countries that do not have such weapon systems. But that may not be a decisive factor. The more important element seems to lie in the fact that the country feels threatened by a hostile force, whether it be a nation or a non-state actor. In this regard, one might argue that in Asia, there are countries which feel threatened seriously. North Korea is an example and so is Iran. In addition, before the peak of the nuclear crises vis-à-vis these two countries, what happened in the subcontinent in 1998 is also a reminder. And yet Israel remains a typical case for a long time. The rationale to choose nuclear weapons lies in the fact that all the existing NWS do not want to give up theirs and that the non-proliferation regime, if only aiming at keeping their nuclear monopoly, will not work.

That said, it must be pointed out that the current non-proliferation regime is the only mechanism that the international community could rely on for controlling the situation. The shortcomings the regime inherently has would have to be addressed by the international society. The common logic is that more NWS would add more risks to the global security. What has happened in the Asia illustrates the situation.

Nuclear stalemate in Asia

Asia is a region where a number of security issues are intermingled. Over the last decade, the United States waged two wars in Asia with its focus on anti-terror campaigns. In West Asia and South Asia, the United States and its allies deployed huge military forces in order to defeat what was perceived by Washington as evil forces. But the mission has not been accomplished. Instead, the United States and western alliance in general have come across persistent resistance, that have caused enormous casualties.

In the case of North Korea, as a political decision, the Kim Jong-Il regime has tried its best to use the nuclear issue to serve its purpose, which is extensively seen as the issue of the regime's survival in the context of perceived attacks by the hostile forces. It is debatable whether North Korea has really developed nuclear bombs in operational sense, but the international community would like to see the development in North Korea as a real threat and the United States tries to tell the world that the nuclear tests by North Korea already present one of the most dangerous challenges to the international community. However, the US proposal to solve the problem may not work, because the United States demands North Korea to end all its nuclear activities and destroy any existing weapons and devices unconditionally and then the United States would have dialogue and cooperation with North Korea. Actually, the South Korean government, after President Lee Myung-bak came to power, has pursued similar policy. Such an approach won't work.

The Six-Party Talks is a bargaining institution, which has played an important role in managing the crisis. Over the past years, relevant parties have tried to get better understanding of each other's positions. Apparently, the talks help all the parties. North Korea's intention to make the bomb, though not acceptable, has to be understood in the context of efforts for survival. One may argue that the regime change could be more desirable to the world. But that does not help solve the problem which is relevant to possession of WMD by the nation. Besides, the governance of North Korea is a domestic issue, not an international issue. The outside world could disagree with the way the regime governs its people, but may not have legitimate rights to force it to change. Unfortunately, the North Korea regime has lived under heavy pressure from outside, at least from their perspectives. The United States classified it into the category of evil states. That makes the regime less confident in holding talks, but more determined to develop WMD as deterrence.

China is deeply worried about the stalemate on the issue. Over the years, China has played a decisive role as host in conducting the talks in the hope that parties may use that forum to share their concerns and reach a consensus on the issue. Checking the progress achieved so far, one has to admit that China's attempts are unsuccessful. Currently, North Korea talks about unconditional resumption of the Six-Party Talks and both the United States and South Korea demand the North to abandon nuclear programs unconditionally before any meaningful talks on the issue could be conducted. The stalemate seems to continue. On the Chinese side, apparently, it is still believed that the Six-Party Talks will be the best option to negotiate and to prevent the dispute from going out of control. Meanwhile, there is a pessimistic feeling that abandonment of the nuclear program by North Korea would be an unrealistic goal.

The Iran nuclear issue looks different. Iran does not admit what it has been doing. Instead, Iran insists on what it calls legitimate use of nuclear energy for civilian purpose. Iranian argument is not convincing and the international community is trying to solve this problem by generating options including coercion. Even though there have been debates in Washington as to whether the United States should use force against Iran, the Obama Administration has been more engaged in how to end the existing wars in the region rather than to start a new one.

As an Asian country, Iran is strategically important. For years, the Iranian nuclear crisis has persisted. Iran uses its position to manipulate the situation, taking advantage of the differences between the big powers. The final solution seems to be a remote prospect. Now that the Arab Spring is drawing more attention, the strategic position of Iran has changed. The issue, as to whether Iran really wants to develop nuclear bombs, looks less important than what Iran is going to do in the changing Middle East. The decline and turbulence of a number of Arabic regimes might help upgrade Iran's position in the region. That is a new variable as far as the Iranian nuclear issue is concerned.

Anti-terror campaign and strategic situation in South Asia

South Asia is an important region for nuclear security in Asia simply because it is a frontier against international terrorist groups and it has concentration of nuclear stockpile. The assumption that the nuclear weapons, if not managed well, could fall into wrong hands is more applicable to South Asia and Pakistan in particular.

Pakistan is a long term victim to international terrorist attacks. After the event of 9/11, Pakistan had to join the US-led war against terror and it is well recognised that Pakistan has made lots of contribution. However, as an Islamic state, Pakistan's cooperation with the United States contains inherent difficulties. Much of the killings and blasts taking place in Pakistan provide the unbearable evidence that Pakistan's engagement in the US-led war is highly risky. But Pakistan does not have much options. After the killing of Osama bin Laden, the inherent difficulties in this regard are increasing and American criticism of the Pakistan government has made the situation more complicated. As a result, there have been lots of assumptions about the future of Pakistan and its nuclear security.

The Pakistani government, both civilian administration and military, does not accept that the nation faces the danger as such. Instead, Pakistani arguments stress that the real problem is the US-led war, which does not have a right strategy, nor does it win the heart of the people in the region. The Pakistani authorities have perfect control over its nuclear stockpiles. Rumours that they might lose control contain motives such as to destroy the credibility of the Pakistani government.

However, the difficult part of the Pakistani issue lies in its relations with the United States, after the death of bin Laden. The difficulty between the two countries has gone so far that the US may attack Pakistan, waging another war in the region. However; that is not believed to be part of the Obama Administration's new strategy because the stake would be too high. From this viewpoint, the nuclear safety in South Asia is highly relevant to the regional stability, in which Pakistan is one of the decisive factors.

Pakistan takes its nuclear deterrence capability as an effective means to safeguard its national security. As long as it believes that strategic balance is to be maintained in the region, there won't be arms race in South Asia. But this belief depends on many factors. Since 1998, the Pakistani strategic community had generally taken for granted that its deterrence capability was convincing and reliable, till the United States and India signed the civilian nuclear deal. That gave a blow to the Pakistani belief of what is known as strategic balance in South Asia. Keeping minimum deterrence vis-à-vis India remains the priority of Pakistani nuclear strategy because there is a deep and increasing asymmetric military situation between the two nations. Now that India has successfully overcome the nuclear isolation imposed by the US-led international community, the implications from this development would enhance more concerns for the Pakistan side. Whether it would stimulate new rounds of arms race is not clear.

China is not a South Asian nation, but China pays great attention to the security situation in the region, because what is going on will affect China in many ways. As for China-Pakistan relations, the traditional values still play an important role in the bilateral relationship, but more importantly, there is a real politik viewpoint. Pakistan shares the border with the Chinese Muslim areas, where the extremist and terrorist groups are a big threat to China's integrity and internal stability. Extremist groups use training facilities in Afghanistan and Pakistan. China and Pakistan have developed effective cooperation for addressing this problem. China's support to the Pakistan government will continue to be backed up with that need in the future. Such support to Pakistan does not and will not aim at any third party. It is aimed at keeping China's periphery stable and opposing any trends that could lead to conflicts and instability. That actually refers to the Chinese approach to Asia-Pacific region and to the world system at large.

Chinese Approaches

China is foremost an Asia-Pacific power with increasing global influence. That determines its behaviour. For instance, China pursues cooperative approaches with other Asia-Pacific players because cooperation will help the region keep its development dynamics and China is both the provider of and beneficiary from the dynamics. For specific issues like nuclear security, arms race and other nuclear related issues, China takes more accommodating approaches, trying to reach consensus with relevant parties. In the meantime, China itself is a nuclear weapon state and what China does will naturally draw attention from the international community and China's own nuclear doctrine.

As a NWS, China has joined nearly all the international treaties and faithfully follows the guidelines of the international norms. Meanwhile, China's nuclear doctrine, since its birth almost half a century ago, remains unchanged. In fact, there have been debates among Chinese researchers on whether it is wise to keep the doctrine as it was even though the situation has changed greatly. One of the debates is about never first use nuclear weapons doctrine. Some argued that it was no longer applicable because conventional weaponry had advanced so much that a nation's defensive capability could be destroyed within very short time as seen during the first and second Iraqi wars. The destruction could include nuclear capabilities, which would imply that adherence to the never first-use-nuclear-weapon doctrine was no longer a valid and wise policy. However, Chinese decision-makers do not show any hesitation in this regard. China will continue to keep its principles, which means that China would resort to nuclear weapons as the last resort when the nation is attacked by nuclear weapons. That example illustrates China's determination to keep its nuclear posture as low as possible. China looks at the nuclear development in the same way as it did half a century ago, despite the collapse of the Soviets. China does not accept the concept that nuclear weapons should only be monopolised by one or two nations and therefore, a complete elimination would be necessary for any real non-proliferation regime. Before that, when nuclear weaponry remains a reality, what responsible nuclear powers can do has to be kept as a political commitment.

Secondly, the existing non-proliferation regime, though unjustified, is the only rational option that the international community has. In this regard, China is expected to continue to follow the spirit and take part, with others, in keeping the current regime as valid as possible. From the Chinese perspective, keeping the regime alive rather than changing its basic principles is better because the international community needs to defend what it proposed before so that the regime could continue to deter potential candidates wanting to take the risk. There are lots of debates about the past failure of the regime and currently, the North Korea case does not show any optimistic signs as far as non-proliferation is concerned. China insists on the mechanism of Six-Party Talks to get North Korea into the process because of China's belief that the non-proliferation regime has to be adhered to.

Thirdly, China never opposes any civilian use of nuclear energy by any country. Believing that civilian use of nuclear energy is an effective way to address energy problems, China supports the international community to implement relevant policies cautiously and that all the countries have legitimate rights to develop civilian programs of nuclear energy. In this regard, China's cooperation with Pakistan has followed the principles of the IAEA. From the Chinese perspectives, the Fukushima crisis, even if putting forward severe warnings about nuclear energy, will not draw a clear line to stop further development of civilian nuclear power because countries are in different situations. Senior Chinese officials already declared that China would not give up nuclear energy. Pakistan has similar difficulties. The shortage of electricity has affected development seriously in Pakistan. China hopes that Sino-Pakistani cooperation will help improve its energy supply and economic development.

Fourthly, in general, China views the nuclear security in Asia with a cautiously optimistic perspective. On the one hand, there are existing security mechanisms that are playing role in crisis management and prevention such as the Six-Party Talks, ASEAN-centred 10 plus forums, Shanghai Cooperation Organisation, etc.. These mechanisms may not provide sufficient solutions to the existing problems, but their role is quite effective in preventing nuclear issues from bursting out into a real crisis. The North Korea nuclear issue sets the example. China will continue to support all the regional institutions for security and in the context of nuclear security, China will stand with the regional organisations to make its own contribution to strengthening them.

On the other hand, as the existing institutions are far from sufficient to strive for a true goal of non-proliferation of WMD, the weaponry is still playing a big role in power politics among big powers. The temptation is huge for non-nuclear states. And for those that are already in the club but have not yet signed relevant treaties, non-proliferation looks more like a trap. They have to observe the obligations of the regime, but it is hard for them to get benefits from it. The observation is thus fragile. To make things worse, there are countries that feel deeply threatened. Countries like North Korea and Iran seem always facing survival challenges from the United States. So far, the existing regime may not be able to cover all the challenges stemming from these complications. In Asia, the situation sends ominous signals that crises, when bursting out, could go out of control. That makes the nuclear situation in Asia a bit dark. China will thus continue to adhere to its traditional policy to stress the importance of reducing the danger of mutual threats existing in Asia through dialogues and negotiations. All the means have to be mobilised to prevent crises. And China will be ready to handle the situation.

Last but not least, China's view on her own national security issue is a mixture of both increasing confidence and caution. From Chinese perspectives, the first and foremost threat to her national security would come from its peripheral areas with the danger of involvement of outside forces. China has pursued a friendly and cooperative periphery policy over the decades, with neighbours. Even though China is surrounded by both existing and potential NWS, China will continue to work with its neighbours for a more reliable framework of regional security architecture. In the meantime, China will continue to host the Six-Party Talks and participate in other dialogue institutions for solutions to potential nuclear issues in Asia. China believes that dialogues and negotiations are the best way to address differences and to eliminate hostilities that are the root causes for the nuclear issues in Asia. The final aim, as far as China's goal is concerned, should be to build up a genuine pan Asian security regime in which all the Asian security events could be dealt with, mainly through the Asians' own efforts.

Conclusion

The nuclear issue in Asia is one of the most dangerous and risky, spawning endless debates and the prospect of large-scale conflicts. The unjustified non-proliferation regime is expected to remain so in the foreseeable future. However, there are increasingly common demands among Asian nations that the region needs a more effective mechanism for regional security. The current talks and relevant institutions for security issues including nuclear ones may provide new opportunity for that process. Now that the Asian security situation has undergone dramatic changes, with the United States strategy shift well under way and also with the rapid rise of developing powers like China and India, the situation requires relevant players to get ready to handle rapid changes in the region. While the decline of the super power together with other western powers is very much debatable and uncertain, it is nevertheless increasingly clear that the major Asian players will take more obligations and responsibilities in handling regional issues including the nuclear issue. With that in mind, one might argue that the day is coming when Asians will be more able to handle Asian affairs through dialogues and cooperation. If that is true, China is expected to build up a new strategy for both regional and global issues.

Session I
Second Paper (Auditorium)

Mr. Tetsuo Kotani (Japan)

Geopolitical Change in Asia and Legal Warfare at Sea: Maritime Asia

Asia is not rising but resurging: Asia was always one of the centres of the world. Asia is growing its economic, financial, technological and political weight in the international system. As Japanese historian Takeshi Hamashita argued, Asia consists of continental and maritime Asia. The former is inward-looking and characterised by agricultural fundamentalism, while the latter is outward-looking and characterised by commercial networks. Today, globalisation has obscured the border between continental and maritime Asia, which creates the dynamism of this region. As Robert Kaplan discussed in his Foreign Affairs article (March/April 2009), on a maritime-centric map of Asia, artificial land borders are becoming obsolete.

Asia faces two great oceans: the Pacific and Indian Oceans. Even landlocked Asian countries are linked with the two Oceans by road, rail, river and pipelines. The Pacific and Indian Oceans should be regarded as a single unified theatre. The offshore island chain in the two Oceans creates a series of marginal seas along the Eurasian continent—including the Sea of Okhotsk, the Sea of Japan, the Yellow Sea, the East and South China Seas, the Andaman Sea, the Bay of Bengal and the Arabian Sea. As geostrategist Nicholas Spykman found out, these marginal seas constitute a "maritime highway" which has contributed to the development of Eurasian coastal areas by providing easy and cheap sea lines of communication.

The geographical term "Asia Pacific" may be insufficient for describing the dynamism in this region. Given the fact that Asia has half the world's population and one-third of the global economy, maritime Asia along the

Indo-Pacific Rim has the potential to reach an unprecedented level of prosperity, freedom and stability in this century. However, this region faces uncertainties as well.

Today, 90 per cent of global commerce and 65 per cent of oil imports travel by sea. Twenty percent of global seaborne trade, 33 per cent of global seaborne crude oil, 37 per cent of global semiconductor trade, 57 per cent of global shipping capacity moves between the Pacific and Indian Oceans via the Malacca Straits. The "maritime highway" linking the Pacific and Indian Oceans constitutes the lifeline of global economy. The seas are important not only as highways but also as suppliers of such marine resources as minerals, energy and food. In short, the dynamism of this region heavily depends on the seas and therefore, future security challenges come from the seas.

Power Shift

Outbreak of piracy is a barometer of hegemonic power. History tells us that piracy thrives when the power of a hegemon declines and continues to flourish until addressed by firm measures. There were no pirates running wild in the Mediterranean during the Pax-Romana, but this Roman inland sea became a piracy hotspot after the fall of the Roman Empire. The North African states, known as the Barbary States, became virtually independent from the declining Ottoman Empire and Barbary corsairs captured American merchant ships and sailors in the Mediterranean that lost the protection of the Royal Navy after the American independence. The United States sent the newly-established Navy and Marines to defeat the Barbary pirates under the slogan "Millions for defence, but not one cent for tribute," and secured the safety of American merchant ships.

Almost two hundred years after the Barbary Wars, the threat of piracy has emerged as a destabilising factor in the maritime domain again. Recent outbreak of piracy in Southeast Asia and then in the Horn of Africa indicates the relative decline of the US sea power. The United States still maintains the strongest navy in the world, but it now has only 282 ships compared with 6,678 in 1945 and 570 in 1990. Given that maintaining one ship on station typically requires three ships—one on maintenance, one on training and one on deployment—the US Navy can never deploy more than 100 ships at sea at any given time and these ships are spread all over the globe. Although the 2007 Cooperative Strategy for 21st Century Sea-power (CS21) aims to maintain credible combat forces in the Western Pacific and the Indian Ocean, these two regions are the world's primary piracy hotspots now.

Under the US-Japan alliance, the United States provides extended deterrence and long-range sea-lane protection for Japan, while Japan provides bases for US armed forces. This alliance structure is premised on US hegemony in Asia. However, the United States is losing its dominance, although it is still an indispensable power. Japan cannot enjoy free and safe sea-lanes any longer under the alliance. Japan is one of the primary beneficiaries of the free trade system under US leadership and needs to contribute to securing the sea-lanes, taking the leadership with the United States in the "1,000-ship" navy.

Throughout its long history, Chinese rulers showed little interest in the seas with some exceptions such as Zheng He's voyages in the 15th century. China became a net oil importer in 1993 and its rapidly growing economy has turned Chinese eyes toward the seas today. Relieved of the Soviet pressure across land borders after the end of the Cold War, China has been investing a lot of resources to build up sea power for energy and sea lane security. The stability of East Asia depends on the balance between land power of China, Russia and India and sea power of the United States and Japan. China's maritime expansion may destabilise this balance. This is literally a sea change.

Chinese maritime expansion began with encircling the resource-rich South China Sea to make it a Chinese lake. After the Philippines kicked out the US Navy from Subic Bay in 1991, Beijing reasserted territorial claims over the Paracel and Spratly archipelagos. Then, China seized Mischief Reef in the Spratlys in 1995.

China is creating a wider strategic buffer in the western Pacific vis-a-vis US Seventh Fleet. Chinese strategy conceived two "island chains" as China's maritime defence barrier. The "first island chain" along the Ryukyus, Taiwan, the Philippines and Borneo is no more than 400 nautical miles from the Chinese coast and China has enhanced anti-access/area-denial (A2/AD) capability up to the "first island chain by purchasing from Russia Su-30 ground-attack aircraft, Kilo-class attack submarines, Sovremmeny-class destroyers with SS-N-22 missiles—all of which the Soviet Union had developed to target US carrier strike groups—spending some one billion dollars annually. China is also introducing Shang-class ultra-quiet nuclear-powered attack submarines. The Chinese Navy has also expanded operational areas into the high seas toward the "second island chain" running along the Bonins and Marianas.

While encircling the South China Sea, China is developing naval facilities (or "pearls") in and diplomatic ties with countries such as Pakistan (Gwadar), Burma (Sittway) and Bangladesh (Chittagong) for sea lane and energy security. This "pearls string" strategy may not be led by Beijing but these Chinese efforts to press on both sides of the Malacca Straits is clearly against strategic interests of Washington. Since its commercial and political interests overlap with China, India also fears being encircled by those "pearls."

Today, the vibrant global economy heavily rests on free and fair access not only to the sea, but also to the air, space and cyberspace. The United States has guaranteed their free and fair use and US military operations also require stability in those global commons. On the other hand, globalisation has proliferated advanced military technologies and doctrines around the world and some states are acquiring asymmetric weapons for a sudden attack against overwhelming US military power. In the Western Pacific, China not only develops conventional weapons such as surface ships, 5th generation fighters and aircraft carriers, but also acquiring asymmetric weapons such as anti-ship ballistic missiles, anti-satellite attack capabilities, advanced sea mines and cyber and information warfare capabilities

Naval Arms Race

The first and largest challenge is naval arms race, stimulated by growing importance of the seas, the decline of US sea power and growing Chinese maritime ambition. Given the relative decline of US sea power and growing Chinese maritime ambition, regional countries from Japan to Southeast Asia and to Australia and India are increasing their naval power, especially power projection capabilities. Several countries have acquired or are acquiring aircraft carriers or large amphibious ships. As Richard Bitzinger pointed out, Asia-Pacific navies are acquiring greater range, speed, operational manoeuvre, firepower, versatility and flexibility. Reflecting this trend, for example, Australian government published a defence white paper calling for reinforcement of sea and air power in 2009. Japan reviewed its mid-term defence policy program in December 2010 and introduced a new concept of "dynamic defence" that will increase the operational level and tempo of Self-Defence Force.

Given the growing importance of the seas, naval arms race will continue in Asia. Submarine build up is the most serious concern. China has almost 60 submarines. But since China lacks reliable anti-submarine warfare capability, regional navies are introducing more submarines. Australia will introduce 12 new submarines. Japan will increase its submarine fleet from 16 to 22. Indonesia has a plan to build 12 submarines to patrol its large sea areas by 2024. India, Singapore, Thailand, Malaysia, Vietnam, South Korea and Bangladesh will also introduce submarines. The sole mission for submarines is sea denial and freedom of navigation in this critical maritime highway is being jeopardized.

Is a naval arms control regime possible in Asia? A model can be the 1922 Washington Treaty. Under the Treaty, the status quo in the Pacific was maintained by arms control and non-fortification agreements. The capital ship tonnage ratio was set among the major naval powers, including United States, Great Britain and Japan. There was a ten-year holiday on capital ship building as well. But no naval arms control regime is feasible today because China has no reason to accept such a mechanism. Also, the problem is Chinese A2/Ad capabilities rather than Chinese naval buildup itself. Overestimation of Chinese naval power is another problem because that intensifies naval arms race in the region. Chinese naval power is still much inferior to US naval power. So the region needs confidence building rather than arms control.

Preserving Good Order at Sea

The second challenge is the preservation of good order at sea. Good order at sea ensures the safety and security of shipping and permits countries to pursue their maritime interests in accordance with agreed principles of international law. Threats to good order at sea include piracy and armed robbery against ships, maritime terrorism, illicit trafficking in drugs and arms, people smuggling, pollution, illegal fishing, marine natural hazards and interstate maritime conflicts.

Piracy and other acts of violence against maritime navigation endanger sea lines of communication and interfere with freedom of navigation and free flow of commerce. Just as the oceans are avenues for global commerce, they are also highways for the import and export of unlawful commodities, including WMD and related materials. Trafficking provides organised crime syndicates, with a huge amount of fund to conduct other crimes or terrorist activities. Intentional acts of pollution or unlawful fishing have negative impact on regional economy and ecosystems. Competition for seabed resources, territorial disputes at sea and environmental nationalism encourage states to exert wider claims over international waters.

The 1982 U.N. Convention on the Law of the Sea (UNCLOS)—the "constitution for the world's oceans"—is the key to good order at sea. It provides a legal and policy architecture for conduct on, over and under the world's oceans as well as a mechanism for peaceful solution of disputes. Freedom of the seas were captured in the grand bargain between the rights of the international community to freedom of navigation and the rights of coastal states to discreet territorial seas and limited jurisdiction beyond the territorial seas.

Preservation of good order at sea requires regional cooperation and leads to confidence building. It is important to note that cooperation among regional coast guards is well advanced. For example, the Japan Coast Guard (JCG) has bilateral agreements with its counterparts in South Korea, China and Russia on coordinated enforcement of illegal fishing and smuggling, rescue and mutual visits of ships and personnel. Bilateral mechanism is important, especially where there are contested waters.

In addition to bilateral cooperation, there are multilateral mechanisms emerging. For instance, coasts guards of Japan, the United States, Russia, Canada, China and South Korea form the annual North Pacific Coast Guard Forum (NPCGF). The NDPGF has become a useful confidence-building mechanism, producing practical outcomes such as joint operational guidelines, combined training for counter-smuggling and fishery enforcement patrol. There is another annual forum called the Head of Asian Coast Guard Agencies Meeting, involving 18 Asian countries to enhance response capabilities for antipiracy and counter-terrorism. Another multilateral mechanism is the ReCAAP (Regional Cooperation Agreement on Combating Piracy and Armed Robbery against Ships), the first intergovernmental anti-piracy agreement adopted by 16 regional countries, including Japan, South Korea, China, India and ASEAN member countries. ReCAAP went into force and an Information Sharing Centre was established in Singapore in 2006.

Confidence building among regional navies remains low-key compared to coast guard cooperation and tends to be influenced by political circumstances. For instance, mutual port calls between the Japanese and Chinese navies was agreed upon in 2000, but the first call was postponed until 2007, due to the deteriorated bilateral relations. The Western Pacific Naval Symposium (WPNS) and the Indian Ocean Naval Symposium (IONS) are the main multilateral mechanisms among regional navies. Interestingly, there are an increasing number of bilateral and multilateral naval exercises among like-minded nations such as Japan, the United States, India, Australia, South Korea, Singapore and Vietnam. These are, in part, a response to Chinese naval assertiveness. Regional navies are also reinforcing cooperation in humanitarian assistance/disaster relief (HA/DR).

On the other hand, transnational efforts to promote greater coastal state jurisdiction, even beyond the national territorial seas, endanger freedom of the seas. This legal warfare or "lawfare"—the efforts to reshape the navigational regimes in UNCLOS and particularly those efforts that have the effect of a diminution of transit passage through international straits and high seas freedoms in the EEZ and high seas—destabilises and weakens the treaty structure.

For example, China is conducting "lawfare" as part of its anti-access strategy. China persists in a series of excessive maritime claims by requiring Chinese approval for innocent passage in the territorial seas by foreign warships or by failing to recognise the airspace above its Exclusive Economic Zone, as international airspace. The US Navy has challenged Chinese "lawfare" under the Freedom of Navigation Program, which led to the Hainan EP-3 incident in 2001 and the recent USS Impeccable incident. The "lawfare" could not only disturb freedom of navigation but also could lead to regional armed conflicts.

China claims the "nine doted," "U-shaped" line in the South China Sea and Chinese "marine surveillance" and "fishery control" boats protect Chinese fishermen while suppressing other countries' fishing boats with threat and even use of force. China has been reluctant to negotiate with other claimants in the South China Sea—Vietnam, the Philippines, Malaysia and Brunei—on a multilateral basis and the 2002 Declaration on the Conduct of Parties in the South China Sea (2002 DOC), the only agreement between ASEAN and China addressing the disputes that is not legally binding. Given recent Chinese assertiveness in the South China Sea, US Secretary of State Hillary Clinton emphasised US interest in freedom of navigation in the South China Sea at the July 2010 ASEAN Regional Forum meeting.

China is also taking assertive actions in the East China Sea. China does not recognise the median line in the East China Sea and claims jurisdiction up to the Okinawa Trough. Although China and Japan reached an agreement on joint development of gas fields along the medium line in 2008, China refuses to make it into a treaty. After Japan arrested the skipper of a Chinese trawler that rammed into Japanese coast guard cutters in Japanese territorial waters around the Senkaku Islands in September 2010, China criticised this and stopped the export of rare earth metals to Japan in retaliation.

Preservation of good order at sea presents both opportunities and challenges. Regional nations should promote cooperation in nontraditional security fields while reaffirming the provisions of the Law of the Sea to preserve good order at sea.

Confidence Building

Confidence building is the third and last challenge, but it is also a solution to the challenges discussed above. Today's naval power plays three key roles: power projection, preservation of "good order at sea," and naval diplomacy/ partnership-building. Naval arms race and "good order at sea" can be managed only through partnership building. There are multiple frameworks and institutions—including US alliance network, WPNS, IONS, Heads of Asian Coast Guard Agencies Meeting, the ReCAAP, ARF and the PSI—which can contribute to maritime security. Multilateral counter-piracy effort off the Somali coast is another example.

Confidence building brings both risks and opportunities. Generally speaking, confidence-building among regional navies has just begun, while regional coast guards are developing substantive cooperation in nontraditional security issues such as counter-piracy. Membership or who to invite makes a difference in partnership building. A partnership can be sometimes hostile to non-members. It is possible that US maritime alliance network and the Shanghai Cooperation Organisation can be opposed to each other. Also, a partnership is ineffective unless key members join. An example is the ReCAAP. Although major powers in this region such as Japan, South Korea, India and China are the members of the ReCAAP, Malaysia and Indonesia have not joined it yet. Some Japanese call for a league of maritime democracies, namely Japan, the United States, India and Australia, based on "common values", but this is not an appropriate approach as long as it excludes China.

Instead, countries in this region should establish a multilateral framework of sea faring nations to avoid naval arms race while preserving good order at sea. Under the framework, member nations should establish crisis management measures and deepen confidence building. Member nations should also deepen cooperation for nontraditional security issues while reaffirming the provisions of the Law of the Sea. In this regard, regional nations should adopt a guideline for military activities on the high seas, reaffirming the UNCLOS provisions, while establishing hot-lines. Regional nations also should reinforce the ReCAAP not only those such as counter-piracy measures but also for other maritime crimes such as terrorism, illegal fishing, smuggling and trafficking.

Each state, even a "rogue" state such as Iran or North Korea, has an intrinsic interest in the effective functioning of the global system of trade, while Al-Qaeda and its associated groups have endemic hostility to the system. Any multilateral framework should be inclusive. There are only two conditions to join into this framework. First, there should be respect for free trade. Second, there has to be respect for freedom of navigation. Regime type does not matter here. The seas are highways, not barriers. China is standing at the crossroads between continental power and sea power. Continental powers regard the seas as barriers, while sea powers regard the seas as highways. China needs to learn that the seas serve best for it when they are regarded as highways.

Then how can such a framework be established? There are at least three layers of multilateral security cooperation. The first layer is a traditional power-based mechanism such as the hub and spokes US alliance network in the region. The second layer comprises of ad-hoc and/or functional mechanisms such as the ReCAAP, the WPNS and the IONS. The third layer is a comprehensive and overall mechanism such as the ASEAN Regional Forum (ARF), the ASEAN Defence Ministers' Meeting Plus (ADMM+), the East Asia Summit and the United Nations.

The first layer mechanism can be used to hedge against any aggression and violation of international law. The second layer mechanism can provide venues for functional cooperation. The third layer mechanism can be used to promote the multilateral framework of seafaring nations. The East Asia Summit is the most appropriate mechanism since it is a summit level forum including all the major players.

Conclusion

Today's geopolitics can be described as a power struggle over EEZs. Ever since the Western powers reached the Far East in the 15th century, the island chains along the Asian continent played an important role in Asian geopolitics. Since those island chains are occupied by independent countries today, China attempts to establish sea control in contiguous seas along the island chains, namely the Yellow Sea, the East and South China Seas and the Philippine Sea. Those seas are EEZs of littoral countries and therefore China conducts "legal warfare" to obtain uninhabited islands as EEZ base points while denying other countries' possession of those islands. China also interprets the Law of the Sea in an arbitrary manner and denies freedom of navigation and over-flight by foreign militaries in its EEZ as part of anti-access strategy. Regional states other than China, such as Vietnam and Malaysia are also making excessive claims in their EEZs.

To ensure regional security, regional states should share the understanding of freedom of the seas and free navigation in EEZ, under UNCLOS. To that end, regional states should launch a "freedom of the seas initiative" under the East Asia Summit. The freedom of the seas initiative can be a venue for regional states to discuss various maritime issues, including the right of free navigation in foreign states' EEZ, law enforcement, marine resource development and marine environmental conservation. The East Asia Summit is an appropriate forum since it brings together the Heads of States. Most urgently, the peaceful resolution of the South China Sea dispute through dialogue and multilateral engagement is crucial for the development of an enduring security architecture in the Asia Pacific Region.

Session I
Third Paper (Auditorium)

Dr Michael Pillsbury (USA)

In Search of China's Strategic Assessment

The problem with contemplating security architectures is that very often it gets mistaken as a way to prevent the occurrence of war. There is a rich legacy of security architectures going back 100 to 500 years; that of building a community of players who reduce misperceptions and arms race and thus avoid war. On the other hand, the realist understanding of International Relations accords importance not to security architectures but to the balance of power among great and small powers.

I have no proposal for any security architecture as such and can indeed understand why such proposals of security architecture are routinely turned down by the governments of countries. The fundamental and irreconcilable problem that keeps such exercises from being successful is that the proposals of individual countries envisage their own selves at the centre of any such architecture.

Thus the focus in this paper would be to stress the importance of understanding the military strategies of various countries in the region. For want of time and opportunity, the paper will be limited to the example of China. Is China really developing itself as the maritime superpower as seen by others? In 2009, a former DIA analyst Cortez Cooper testified before the US Congress that the US could potentially dissuade China from its decision to build increasingly formidable maritime power projection capabilities.

Ranking Strategic Priorities

According to Rand Corporation estimates, between 2011 and 2025, China would be spending 490 billion and 500 billion dollars respectively on their air force and navy. This is very less considering the amount of resources China has, at its disposal and that China could build a larger power projection force. Any security architecture in the region should focus on preventing precisely such a build-up. One way of trying to achieve this is by assuring China against threats from its neighbours. There are opposing views on whether it is actually possible to ask China to scale down its current military capabilities.

One striking feature of the region is that while countries are interested in keeping a close watch on and pre-empting Chinese moves, unlike the USA, there is very little effort to purchase and translate Chinese books and documents on defence policy, to try and understand what China is thinking. The assessment presented here culls from six major Chinese sources. They are – Military training plans in books, Chinese leaders' public statements, television reports of military exercises, television programs on military forces, military authors' analyses in open journals and advocacy in military books.

In 2007, President Hu Jintao announced that he wanted the military to set itself four missions. While they are not publicly released, the PLA is known to have renewed focus on acquiring resources for the navy, airborne missiles, space and cyber technologies and its bases.

Fifteen Fears

As culled from Chinese military literature, there are some major threats that China perceives for itself and therefore develops its military capacities towards meeting those threats. Fifteen threats are listed in the succeeding paragraphs.

1. **Overseas resources** – China sees itself blockaded by a series of Island chains, led by Japan. To appreciate this fear, one needs to think about India's outlet to the Indian Ocean blockaded by island fortifications by Pakistan.

2. **Encroachment through sea** - The fear is against the plundering of resources by other countries. The reports of attacks on Chinese

fishing boats by external navies in South China sea have been widely circulated. Its coastal army also remains worried.

3. **Protecting Sea Lines of Communication (SLOC)** – This is a relatively minor concern.

4. **Fear of land invasion** - China is more scared of invasion from land and spends most of its military resources there. 70 per cent of Chinese forces are ground forces. Also the largest military exercises in recent times involved armour and airborne units. A Chinese book published in 2005 analyses how the army visualises seven regions of the country to be at threat from land invasion. Each region has unique geographies and faces different nation-states. They, in turn have dedicated defence infrastructure and are encouraged to be creative in preparing for countering invasion. A summary of apprehensions in some of the regions is given below.

   (a) Nanjing Military Region.

       (i) Invasion from Taiwan.

       (ii) Perceived inability to seize Taiwan if called upon to do so.

       (iii) Should the PRC decide to invade Taiwan, the US may intervene.

   (b) Guangzhou Military Region. Confrontation in South China Sea may take place with the following countries who have staked claim.

       (i) Vietnam.

       (ii) Philippines.

       (iii) Malaysia.

       (iv) Indonesia.

(c) Chengdu Military Region. Major apprehensions are as under :-

   (i) Operations against India. Arms race in the Himalayan complex has been triggered. Secondly, Artillery nuclear deployments and simulation exercises have been conducted. Deployment in Tibet Autonomics Region has been strengthened.

   (ii) Instability in Burma. Visits by senior leaders from the US and India to Burma are raising suspicions in China.

   (iii) Differences with Vietnam. Should events take a serious turn, the US may support Vietnam.

(d) Lanzhou Military Region. Major fears are as under :-

   (i) Should North and South Korea unify, China will loose a reliable ally in North Korea. A unified Korea on the border is bound to pose a formidable threat.

   (ii) Danger of Korean crisis leading to war which may go nuclear.

   (iii) Japanese military build up and alliance with South Korea. Both countries have the potential of going nuclear at short notice and can be formidable opponents.

   (iv) Japanese alliance with India. It may lead to operations on more that one front concurrently.

   (v) Loss of Russian support and imbalance of power in Asia.

(e) Beijing Military Region. Some of the apprehensions are as under :-

   (i) Mongolian animosity and pro-west drift.

   (ii) Loss of capital to Russian invasion or revolt from within or a combination of the two.

(iii) Russian alliance shift to the USA.

(iv) The US stealth air attacks via Korea and Yellow Sea.

The thrust of the military preparedness in each of these seven regions is not global power projection on land or on sea, but protection from invasion.

5. **Fear of armour attack.** 'Northern Sword' Exercise of 2005 betrays a concern for armoured invasion. Exercise involved 20,000 personnel, elements of 2800 tanks and two tank divisions. The Chinese threat perception of land attack considered an attack from one end of its landmass to the other.

6. **Instability, riots and civil war.** A series of exercises have been conducted by the military in this regard. A new decision-making unit has been set up and media has reported at least ten counter terrorism exercises. Chinese military literature considers India as an aggressive and powerful force in the region, a 'sub-hegemon' of sorts that backs up Tibetan protests and riots. Many analyses suggested the breaking up of connection between India and Tibetan dissidents. Other major army exercises focussed on anti riot operations which envisaged internal riots orchestrated by outside power.

7. **Fear of attack on pipelines.** This is a development of the past decade or so and has a low priority for the military. Since 2001, there have been annual exercises for pipeline defence and there is strong demand for the deployment of additional forces for the purpose. To overcome energy chokepoints, Burma is considered as an opportunity to break island chain and resolve the Malacca dilemma.

8. **Fear of aircraft carriers.** China has carried out operations research studies of aircraft carriers, positioned south of Taiwan. There are several programs on anti-ship ballistic missiles and advocacy on how to attack US carriers with various weapons employing different

tactics.

9. **Fear of air-strikes.** The Chinese army has received large amounts of equipment over the past decade, including AAA guns, surface to air missiles and logistic support equipment. It is understood that one third of the Army's reserve divisions are AAA units. Air defence missions are shared by a set of organisations, including surface to air missile forces, AAA forces, radar troops as well as fighter aviators.

10. **Fear of Taiwan's loss to foreign powers.** While the international community thinks that the fulcrum has shifted towards Chinese influence, the Chinese government is itself not too confident. Chinese analysts still cannot guarantee that foreign power won't use Taiwan to invade China and is concerned about the threat of war if the Taiwan situation spins out of control.

11. **Insufficient forces to unify Taiwan.** In this regard, in recent years expenditure has been directed towards closing the gap in infrastructural development, logistical facilities, transportation routes and naval bases.

12. **Fear of attacks on missile forces by preemption, commandoes, jamming and air-strikes.** China's 2nd artillery operation force training employs the simulation of 'blue force' or 'enemy' Threats of attacks by special forces or commando raids on command centres, electromagnetic jamming and network attacks using hackers and computer viruses are of concern. The Wall Street Journal reports on one of China's most expensive and innovative initiatives- a 3000 mile underground tunnel network with missile capabilities. Such a measure would be too expensive and unwieldy anywhere else, even by US standards.

13. **Fear of escalation of conflict and loss of control.**
    Chinese military authors have often expressed concerns about 'war

control' by the military. The general consensus is that if crisis escalates, the first battle is decisive. Springing unexpected 'assassin mace' weapons and throwing the enemy out of control is preferred. To prevent loss of control China is investing heavily, including the developing of offshore command and control capacities.

14. **Fear of cyber attacks, network leakage.** Failure to construct secure systems and cover channels are often raised. Flaws in systems may lead to loss of control of war. Efforts to keep abreast is a continuous ongoing process.

15. **Fear of attacks on ASAT capacities.** A lot of attention is also paid to the development of anti-satellite forces. Chinese doctrine stresses the need to keep their deployments covert, assuming that if it was known that they had anti-satellite missile capabilities, these would be destroyed first. It also stresses the need to persuade all other countries not to develop anti-satellite forces. Some chinese books also recommend that ASAT would be effective only if it was used to surprise the opponent with 'shock and awe', in space. The 2007 action of pulling down their own weather satellite and subsequent refusal to explain their actions to the international community can be understood in this light.

Since China's public declaratory policies are designed to be ambiguous, it is very important to understand China's strategic assessment of the future through Chinese eyes. Their military development is more geared to address geopolitical challenges rather than contributing towards a security architecture. The challenges for the international community would be to find ways to persuade China to have limited military forces like that of Germany and Japan, post 1945. It is important to understand what would drive China to keep focussing inwards or to develop global power projection. Any enduring security architecture for the region needs to engage with these concerns.

Session I (Seminar Room 1)
Chairman's Opening Remarks
Mr Fyodor Lukyanov (Russia)

First of all, I would like to express my gratitude to be able to come to Delhi and participate in this seminar, which I think is of enormous importance to everybody present. To me, it is especially interesting because Russia, being a primarily Asian country with 77 per cent of its territory located therein, is still a new-comer on the scene. Its foreign policy engagement, till very recently, had been focussed only on the West. To me, the seminar is also a very interesting research study; to listen to my colleagues and understand what the outstanding security concerns of the region are. We have some distinguished panelists present today. I am privileged to pass the floor on, first of all, to Prof Bharat Karnad, whose paper on nuclear issues is a very pertinent one to start with.

Session I
First Paper (Seminar Room 1)

Professor Bharat Karnad

Strategic and Nuclear Balancing of China in the Asia-Pacific

Synopsis

> The security situation in the Asia-Pacific is unsettled by the perceived decline of American power and the continued ascent of China to dominating status in Asia. All the countries bordering China (except, perhaps, Pakistan which, in any case, is no part of the Asia-Pacific scene) have territorial disputes with it on land and sea. The shared threat perception has led to major Asia-Pacific countries, in particular India, United States and Japan, seeking military and strategic cooperation with each other and with the littoral states of the ASEAN, fearful of Chinese designs, particularly on the disputed but natural resource-rich South China Sea, despite their economic and trade links with China. The antidote to contain and constrain China in the security sphere is for the countries of this extended region to firm up programs of military collaboration in crises, which do exist but need further strengthening. In this correlation of forces, while the conventional military forces of the US and India and of the countries on China's periphery do matter, the strategic nuclear capabilities of the US and India are as central to deterring China and maintaining peace and stability in the extended region as are the Japanese and Taiwanese nuclear weapons projects in embryo.

The new millennium is turning out to be everything nobody expected it to be. The international power shift from the Atlantic world to Asia has spawned uncertainty and deepened insecurities and mistrust, even as terrorism and economic blight have spread virally. It has fuelled, in some Asian countries, paranoia and in others, the resolve to protect national interests with whatever mix of political and military policies that promise a modicum of order and stability in the region. The convergence of the two streams has led to enormous flux in policy where every country is at once hedging and manoeuvring for slivers of advantage.

These developments, moreover, are in the larger context of an economically vibrant China throwing its weight around, so far mostly in Asia, while playing the banker to a heavily indebted United States as well as the European Union (EU); an exhausted America, apparently drained of self-confidence and resources, trying desperately to hang on to its dominant status even as it attempts to deal with the massive war-expenditure induced economic recession and attendant high rates of unemployment; an increasingly irrelevant and diffident EU, habituated to riding the US coat-tails in all areas, is contributing marginally to the US-led NATO missions (Afghanistan, Iraq, Libya), while many of its members (Greece, Italy, Spain and Portugal) face bankruptcy and a future in which, not Washington, but Beijing is the economic "saviour"; and, the countries in East Asia, South-East Asia and in the Indian Ocean littoral, face a China that is not a distant entity, even less an abstract 'celestial economy', but a relentlessly driven power, hungry for hegemonic substance, standing and recognition and perceived by almost all other Asian states as imperiling their security and peace of mind and, therefore, requiring counter-balancing with a cautiously willing United States and a hesitant India.

In such a milieu, what the majority of Asian countries are looking for is reassurance, overlapping guarantees of security from whatever credible sources may be available. Counterveiling strategic alliance or partnership with the United States and/or India, both countries nuclear-armed and with strategic heft and ostensible rivals of and in sometimes tense relationship with, China, is the policy choice of most of these states. A few of them, while tacking to these winds, are also surreptitiously nursing the capability to produce nuclear weapons just in case it is ever needed. The nuclear-armed regime of Kim Jong Il in North Korea, by successfully warding off the US for over a decade, has proved that the bomb guarantees its owners, protection from molestation by a big power, under all circumstances.

This paper will briefly analyse a couple of inter-connected issues: (1) the attitude and posture, vis-a-vis China, of the United States and of India, as perceived by Asian states on the Chinese periphery; smaller Asian countries hope to rely on these two powers to blunt China's growing power and (2) considering the difficult security situation, Japan, Taiwan, Vietnam and other ASEAN states find themselves, in the strategic policy choices they are making in terms of cultivating and strengthening politico-military ties, with the United States and India. The paper concludes that the strategic and nuclear counter-balancing of China will be the background in which inter-state relations will play out in Asia, in the foreseeable future.

Litmus Test States

Japan and Taiwan are among the oldest and staunchest allies of the United States, in Asia – their links forged at the start point of the Cold War between Soviet Russia-led Communist bloc of nations and the so-called Free World headed by the US. The security of these two states, both cowering in the shadow of an increasingly aggressive China, has been the lynchpin of America's Far East policy. Any perceived weakening of the US security commitment to either country is seen as the bellwether of Washington's lack of resolve to stay anchored in Asia. As it is, Taiwanese and Japanese confidence was shaken by the entente engineered by the Nixon-Kissinger duo and the Shanghai Declaration that eventuated in 1972. For the first time, the US acknowledged Taiwan not as a separate, sovereign entity but, more ambiguously, as part of the "One China, two systems" concept.

The US intent was to use Mao Tse Tung's China to balance the Soviet Union. To firm up the value of this geostrategic card, Washington transferred military high technology to gild China's military muscle and opened up the American market to Chinese exports – an opportunity the far-sighted

Chairman Deng Xiaoping quickly capitalised on to get the country's economy rolling on the exports-driven path. The rapprochement, however, ended up leaving Taiwan in the lurch, its security concerns that the US sought to address with the 1979 Taiwan Relations Act, promising protection, in case Beijing tried forceful means of "unification". Joining the international mainstream has resulted in sustained skyrocketing growth for China, averaging some 9 per cent annually over the last 30 years and an economy set to overtake the US as early as 2015, but no later than 2020. Taiwan, ironically, played a leading role in China's economic regeneration. It is responsible for over 80 per cent of Foreign Direct Investment in China, with Taiwanese industrialists and entrepreneurs exploiting the low wages and state subsidies to establish that country as a base for exporting low cost manufactures to a global market and establishing China as the "workshop of the world". Beijing, on its part, has all along hoped that such linkages would, over time, ease Taiwan's peaceful absorption into the larger Chinese fold. But the most significant development is not that Taiwan and China are mutually dependent but that, notwithstanding the enormous economic gains accruing to Taiwan, the sentiment for resolutely maintaining its status, independent of and separate from China's, continues to be strong and animates much of Taiwanese politics.

Indeed, the leader of the opposition, that is, the Democratic Progressive Party's (DPP) Tsia Ing-wen's call, during her September 2011 visit to Washington, for a new basis for US-Taiwan relations and the possibility, moreover, of her winning the general elections in January 2012 has sent unease coursing through Washington and Beijing because of their shared fear that Sino-US relations and the region, generally, may be heading, once again, for a rough ride. When DPP last ruled in Taipei, President Chen Shui-bian, it may be recalled, had mooted a nation-wide referendum on independence and precipitated a China-US confrontation in the mid-1990s in the Taiwan Straits. In more recent times, the US Government's faint-hearted approach to helping Taiwan strengthen its armed forces may have placated Beijing but it has, apparently, discouraged not just the Taiwan nationalists such as Tsia but also the ruling Kuomintang Party, which would prefer that Taiwan stay engaged with China but also remain a distinct entity, to achieve which goal, periodic injections of advanced weapons systems into the island state, to counter the arms build-up on the Mainland, are necessary.

Three requests by Taipei, since 2006, to replace 66 of its aging F-16 A/Bs from a fleet of 150 such planes with the newer F-16 C/Ds, were hanging fire for over five years before the Obama Administration finally turned them down. Instead, only a mere upgrading of the existing Taiwanese F-16 A/Bs in a pared down deal worth $4.2 billion was approved, which will do nothing to correct a major skewing of the air warfare capabilities in China's favour. The PLA Air Force units fronting on Taiwan are outfitted with Su-27s, Su-30s, J-10s and even the fifth generation J-20 combat aircraft. A US Congressional assessment, surveying the scene has observed that, "the US paralysis over sales of these aircraft since 2006 has given China time to develop more advanced capabilities...and evaluate capabilities to defeat even more advanced US tactical aircraft such as the F-22". A relieved Beijing said little unlike its response to President Barack Obama's 2010 announcement of a $6.4 billion arms package, that included missiles, Black Hawk helicopters and mine-sweepers, when it went ballistic.

Washington's room for manoeuvre and in fact, its ability to take a strong stand on Taiwan's autonomy is limited by the current economic depression and high unemployment that the US is experiencing, combined with the resource-draining wars in Iraq and Afghanistan that it is embroiled in. While President Obama is beginning to wind down these wars, it is unlikely that there will be significant cost savings, considering US Special Forces' presence will continue in the more active theatre, Afghanistan, for a long time and periodic injections of huge amounts of money into Pakistan will be required, as incentive to keep Islamabad from bolting the "global war on terrorism". The US condition will not be helped by Beijing continuing to buy US Treasury bonds so that its exports to the American market remain at a high level. It is the recognition of limited options America has that led US Vice President Joseph Biden, on his return from a state visit to China, to state categorically that Washington does not entertain "visions of a cold war-style rivalry or great power confrontation with China." In the context of "China's growing military abilities and intentions", he volunteered, the

US is "engaging with the Chinese military to understand and shape their thinking." The trouble is that it may be China that is actually "shaping" US thinking on Asia and not the other way around, especially because American strategic experts, having conceded a "power shift", seem to have already thrown in the towel.

Security-wise, Japan finds itself in much the same unenviable position as Taiwan, caught between the economic pull of China and the security pull of the US. The new Democratic Party government was elected on the promise that it would reconsider that country's US-centred foreign and military policy. Once in office, however, Prime Minister Yoshihiko Noda has tried to find the middle ground between two policy streams – one tending to China, the other to the United States. The European Union-inspired concept of an East Asian Community proposed by a former premier from his Party, Yukio Hatoyama in 2009, as a means of solidifying the burgeoning economic linkages with China, was in the backdrop of his failure to convince the US Government to reduce the major US military presence in and move the American base to a less populated part of Okinawa. The other stream was the hard line adopted by his immediate predecessor, Naoto Kan, in the long simmering territorial dispute over the Senkaku/Diaoyu island chain. It resulted, in 2010, in an incident at sea leading to the Japanese navy arresting and releasing a captain of a Chinese vessel that occasioned a volley of harsh words by Beijing.

Japan's Self-Defence Forces, boasting of significant anti-submarine warfare and air superiority capabilities, an air assault brigade and a navy bigger than most big power navies, are more than competent to handle China by themselves in the conventional military realm. As backstop is the US 7th Fleet in Yokohama, the forward-based American air strike and combat elements and the land force contingent on Okinawa, which are bound, willy nilly, to get involved in any Japan-China military clash. But over and above that is the status of Japan as a "para-nuclear state" that can, in no time at all, convert vast holdings of reprocessed spent fuel plutonium from its many power plants into quite literally "thousands of nuclear warheads" to deter Chinese threats, as Ichiro Ozawa, the Liberal Party president warned in 2002. He went on to boast that "If we get serious, we will never be beaten in terms of military power." This kind of uncharacteristically incautious utterance by a Japanese leader may mirror the rethink going on in Japanese security circles about self-reliance, owing to doubts about US as a reliable military ally. It is a feeling that has been further fuelled by Washington deciding not to sell 40 F-22 Raptors that Tokyo had asked for, even before the decision was taken to scrap that aircraft program. Even the deal for the F-35 Joint Strike Fighter for Japan in lieu of the F-22 is minus some of the cutting edge stealth capabilities. It is the sort of attitude that does not inspire confidence. Similar doubts motivated the South Korean nuclear weapons program, started in the 1974 by President Park Chung Hee that Washington pressured Seoul into abandoning, but which went covertly ahead anyway; it, however, progressively lost steam.

Unlike Japan, Taiwan has a small and effective "Hsin Chu" nuclear weapons program at the Chungsan Institute of Science and Technology, initiated in the wake of the Chinese atomic test in October 1964. In the 1970s, CIA was of the view that this program could produce a nuclear bomb inside of five years. Some forty years later, it is reasonable to assume they have ready nuclear warheads for the two strategic nuclear-capable missiles developed as part of the so-called "Tiching Project". The missiles are a 1000 km range, two stage, solid fuel variant and another with range of 300 kms, both designed to carry the same sized nuclear warhead. In essence then, Taiwan too has a nuclear deterrent, in embryo, to fall back on. Nevertheless, by way of abundant caution and to keep any conflict on this side of the nuclear Rubicon, the clause invoking US military protection in the Taiwan Relations Act is likely to be invoked by Taipei at the first hint of serious trouble with China, despite Taiwan's quite considerable conventional military preparedness. As the latest US Department of Defence report on the Chinese military capabilities clearly states, other than the small sparsely populated offshore islands, "An attempt to invade Taiwan would strain China's untested armed forces", "pose a significant political and military risk" for Beijing and in light of "Taiwan's investments to harden infrastructure and strengthen defensive capabilities", make it difficult for China "to achieve its objectives."

It is now evident that Tokyo and Taipei, looking beyond the US strategic umbrella, are seeking to add more arrows to their defensive quiver. India is a country both states hope will join them in their separate endeavours, so far exclusively underwritten by the US military deployment, to fence in China. The Indian Navy has been exercising frequently with the Japanese Navy in the waters off Senkaku and with the navies of South Korea, Vietnam, Singapore and other ASEAN members. While Delhi put off the "trialogue" with Japan and the United States in 2011, lest China see this as a formal ganging up by rival powers, it has been forthcoming in the military field – conducting the annual 'Malabar' naval exercise, most recently in summer 2011, with a destroyer flotilla off Okinawa alongside the US naval forces, an exercise the Japanese Navy had to withdraw from, owing to its preoccupation with the Fukushima nuclear disaster relief work. One reason why India and Japan are increasingly on the same page as far as China is concerned, is perhaps because Beijing is employing the same strategy with both countries, of testing their defences with provocative acts. Incursions across the disputed Sino-Indian border (Line of Actual Control) by the Chinese PLA and the paramilitary People's Armed Police units and the air space by Chinese helicopters are, apparently, as common now as the 96 incidents (a tripling of such violations over the past year) of intruding Chinese aircraft intercepted by Japanese air defence fighter planes over the outer Japanese islands.

Even so, Delhi appears diffident, which problem was sought to be addressed in 2010 by the visiting former Japanese Prime Minister, Shinzo Abe, who likened Japan's situation to that of India in its relations with China and advised Delhi not to feel "shy" in joining the United States and Japan to keep the Asian sea lanes open and safe, because such military cooperation will soon draw other Asian states, such as Vietnam and South Korea into a collective security enterprise. He counselled that India and Japan ought to work together to ensure that, in this time of US weakness, there is "no strategic void" and, by implication, that this void is not filled by China. Abe also indicated the direction in which the mutually compatible countries are headed, saying "India's success is in Japan's best interests and Japan's success is in the best interest of India." Japan has also overcome its earlier reservations about conducting nuclear trade with India, making the distinction between a nuclear weapon state and a nuclear proliferator. This trend of greater Japanese strategic engagement with India is reflected in strengthening economic bonds, such as Japan emerging as the sixth largest source of Foreign Direct Investment.

India's links with Taiwan are still a work in progress, but proceeding along the lines that the two countries have generally agreed upon. Taiwanese Member of Parliament Chen Chiech-Ju, visiting Delhi in October 2011 as head of a DPP delegation, proposed greater cooperation between littoral states, including India, to contain Chinese expansionism and maritime ambitions. The Indian government, while happy with such sentiments, is more focussed on getting a big part of the Taiwanese Foreign Direct Investment, presently channeled into the Mainland, diverted to India. But Taipei's efforts in pushing such diversion of capital have floundered because the Taiwanese businessmen and industrialists find the difficulties of language and the poor quality of infrastructure in India, obstacles that are too big to easily overcome. This reluctance is despite some singular successes racked up by Taiwanese Companies in India, such as Acer Computers and the telecommunications firm, D-Link. Early in the last decade, India broached the subject of sharing intelligence on China with Taiwan, given Taipei's effective intelligence penetration of the Chinese system. The Taiwanese were however skeptical about what they would get, of value, in return. But, as Antonio Chiang, former Deputy Secretary General, National Security Council, Taiwan, who visited Delhi a number of times in the last decade, said in 2006: "Both sides have felt good about each other but are still unsure about what to do." Some of those early doubts may have been settled and cooperation, mostly in the intelligence field, is underway. More substantive cooperation, starting with joint exercises, in the security field may follow.

South-East Asia: China's Soft under-belly

For geographically obvious reasons, South East Asia at once confronts China with danger and opportunities. The littoral states, while wishing to benefit from the surging Chinese economic growth, are nevertheless wary of Chinese intentions and Beijing's moves are invariably looked upon with suspicion. The strategic problem for China is that one of its two most volatile regions,

Tibet (the other being Xinjiang) is proximal to this region and harsh Chinese Communist rule and oppression of Tibetan people and Tibetan culture are seen as warning signals of the overarching danger posed to South East Asian states by China. The fear inspired by proximity to China has prompted increased defence expenditures and military acquisitions. Malaysia's military acquisitions budget, for example, has gone up by some 700 per cent in the 2005-2010 period, Singapore's by 140 per cent and Indonesia's by 84 per cent. Even so, the ASEAN states are not comfortable and seek further bolstering of their security by looking to India, with size, location and politico-military weight, to act as shield and counter. Unfortunately, the Indian government has lacked the strategic vision and the drive sufficient enough to cash in on the anxiety triggered in this region by a China fast emerging as a great power.

To that extent, India's 'Look East' policy has succeeded other than in fostering trade and commercial ties with the countries of that region, it has been in the slow and substantive buildup of security partnerships across South East Asia, led by naval diplomacy. The leading countries with which India is developing special security relationships are Singapore, Malaysia, Indonesia and particularly Vietnam. The annual 'Milan' naval exercise involving the ASEAN (Association of South East Asian Nations) members and Bangladesh, Maldives, et al, with portions of the on-shore interaction designed to cultivate social bonding between the sailor communities and, at higher levels, allowing officers to exchange views on the evolving military situations they face and to chalk out cooperative and collaborative counter measures. Such confidence building programs have prompted greater mutual reliance. Thus, Singapore sent its submarine crews to train on Indian ex-German HDW 209 Submarines, also in service with the Singapore Navy and its Air Force regularly uses Indian air space for training purposes. The Malaysian Air Force pilots flying ex-Russian Mi-29 aircrafts and the maintenance crews servicing these planes, are trained by the Indian Air Force. Along with other ASEAN countries, Vietnam sends scores of its senior officers for higher command training to India's National Defence College and depends on the Indian Armed Services for technical support. Delhi finally accepted the logic, that has been articulated for many years now, of arming Vietnam with consequential weaponry and the strong pitch by Vietnam and Indonesia for the Indian Brahmos supersonic cruise missile. As a result, this missile may soon be found on Vietnamese and Indonesian warships and outfitting their coastal batteries, no doubt to the considerable unease of the Chinese South Seas Fleet operating out of Sanya base on Hainan Island. South China Sea may no longer be exclusively China's sea as Beijing perceives it with its rather arbitrary drawing of the expansive U-shaped dotted line on maps to claim most of it, a sea territory rich in oil and gas and hence even more vigorously contested by neighbouring countries, including Malaysia, Vietnam, Brunei and the Philippines.

India is seen by these states as a counter-balancing military presence to China in the extended area, especially with the US naval forces in the strategic mix, securing the eastern end of the arc of the Chinese periphery in Asia-Pacific in league with the Japanese and Australian defence forces. The Indian government's continued hesitation in overtly making common cause against China hasn't prevented the Indian Navy from participating in joint manoeuvres with its US, Australian and Japanese counterparts. Much of the firming up of the collective effort to ring in China is despite most of the countries, including India, having strong trade and economic relations with it. China displaced the United States two years ago as India's largest trading partner, with trade growth exceeding targets. The other states bordering China similarly are plugged into the Chinese manufacturing loop, such as Vietnam and Thailand, or are prime exporters of natural resources (wood, minerals, oil, off shore gas) to meet Chinese industrial demand, such as Myanmar. But all of them share the same high level of distrust where China is concerned, owing to historical memory of imperial Chinese aggression and, in many instances, unresolved border disputes and because of their apprehension of once again being reduced to vassal or tributary status. Some of these countries, in particular Myanmar, expressly blame India for "pushing" it "into Chinese arms" by over-stressing the Human Rights angle, but have quickly grasped the Indian offer of development aid and military assistance to balance the Chinese presence. This, even though Myanmar has allowed a rapid north-south road and rail build-up, enabling China to to have an opening on the Bay of Bengal through a deep water port it is constructing on the offshore Ramree Island.

China's claims on the South China Sea, encompassing the disputed Spratly and Paracel Island chains and coveted by many of the other nearby states because of rich oil and gas deposits found in those areas, have been arbitrary, transgressing existing maritime laws and conventions. Notwithstanding its being party to the 2002 ASEAN Declaration on Conduct (DOC) of countries with claims on South China Sea, Beijing warned all countries to terminate oil exploration and drilling activities, not specifically permitted by it. Oil majors, such as Exxon and British Petroleum were intimidated enough to cease operations. China's expansive offshore territorial claims have been vigorously challenged, in legal terms, by Vietnam. Hanoi has complained about China's non-conformance with numerous 1982 UNCLOS (United Nations Convention on the Laws of the Sea) provisions. Elsewhere, Philippines upped the ante when Chinese aircrafts and naval vessels tried to run its people off the Reed Bank in the Paracels, by totally rejecting Chinese claims and invoking the 1951 Mutual Defence Treaty with the United States in order to deter China from taking precipitate action. A defensive Beijing fell back on justifying its claims on the basis of these being "formed by history". It led to the US Secretary of State Hillary Clinton at the ASEAN summit, in Hanoi, committing America to, in effect, enforcing the international maritime law.

Vietnam, in furtherance of its proactive stance, also cleverly triggered both an acknowledgement, by Delhi, of a naval encounter off its coastline with China in order, presumably, to gauge India's resolve to back Vietnam and to test its willingness to protect its energy stake. Having earlier accorded the Indian Navy the right to use the port of Nha Trang on the South China Sea as provisional base whenever its ships are in the vicinity, Vietnam leaked the details of a mid-July 2011 encounter that the Indian navy amphibious assault ship, INS Airavat, sailing north to Haiphong, had with a suspected Chinese ship, in which Airavat was ordered out of those waters. The Indian ship did nothing of the kind and the incident made it to the international Press almost a month later. Critical commentaries in Indian newspapers resulted in the Indian Ministry of External Affairs departing from its usual policy line of offering China minimum offence and asserting India's right, in a joint venture with Vietnam, to drill for oil in an area clearly within Vietnamese claim lines. Hanoi, it may be deduced, hoped to test the seriousness of Delhi's profession of support for its South China Sea claims in particular and its readiness to tangle with the Chinese naval forces and, presumably, was delighted with the outcome, what with India providing proof of being a reliable strategic partner. Vietnam and India categorically rejected the Chinese exclusive claim on the South China Sea with India making it clear that the state owned oil exploration firm – ONGC Videsh Ltd, would continue to explore and exploit its resource-rich seabed. In fact, the new found bounce in bilateral relations can be seen in the 13 Oct 2011 joint statement, issued during the state visit to India, of the Vietnamese President, Truong Tan Sang, which repeatedly harped on their "strategic partnership". China is watchful and believes that the move to involve India in the South China Sea disputes was actually instigated by Vietnam and the Philippines and that, under the circumstances, it may be best to be more confrontationist. Beijing is considering replacing its policy of "shelv[ing] the dispute and joint[ly] develop[ing]" the oil and gas fields, with one that "must dare and ...develop" and otherwise draw "an insurmountable red line" which, it hopes, an "ambitious" but "immature" India will not cross, especially in the context of "reluctant" United States and Japan.

The "string of pearls" to-date may be more potential than reality. But it does show China's long term plan to avoid the possible Malacca choke point by developing other trade and access routes via construction of deep water ports on the Indian Ocean littoral, such as Ramree Island in Myanmar and Gwadar on the Baluch coast in Pakistan.

Conclusion

The strategic worries and insecurities sparked by the aggressive Chinese policy and the uncertainties attending on the best way to handle a growingly uncontrollable China, manifestly the dominant Asian power, suggest the obvious hedging strategy for countries of Asia-Pacific, desirous of constraining China. This strategy will have to rely on the US, Indian and

Japanese militaries, their combined capabilities augmented by the military wherewithal and locational attributes of smaller countries in the region. The objectives would be to, firstly, strengthen the choke capabilities at the Malacca Straits with India's integrated Andaman military command in the van; secondly, to reject the exclusionist Chinese notions of "closed sea" whether in the South China Sea environs or in the Yellow Sea area and, finally, collectively to get into a position to mobilise and deploy sufficient naval, air, land and strategic nuclear forces in relatively quick time, to dissuade and deter Beijing from embarking on provocative or punitive military actions against any single state or set of countries in the Asia-Pacific region.

Session I
Second Paper (Seminar Room 1)

Sr Col Tran Hau Hung (Vietnam)

The Security and Strategic Environment in the Asia Pacific

The Asia-Pacific accounts for 40 per cent of total land area, 41 per cent of population (nearly 3.6 billion people), 62 per cent of GDP, 47 per cent of trade value and 48 per cent of FDI of the world. The Asia-Pacific has an important geo-strategic position with many economically vital sea lanes linking Pacific and Indian Oceans. The Asia-Pacific encompasses dynamically and rapidly developing economies. Many powers have strategic interests in the region. Thus, the region gains special attention of many countries. The Asia-Pacific has 65 per cent of global raw materials and some important sea lanes of the world. Asia Pacific gathers many powers of the world, including the world's 3 biggest economies (US, China and Japan) and 3 out of 5 UNSC permanent members (US, China and Russia). Despite effects of the economic crisis, the regional economic development remains the world's fastest, with an average annual growth of 7.5 per cent. There are rapid changes in the regional context, creating both opportunities and challenges for regional countries.

Shifts in the power balance and the multi-polarisation

Asia-Pacific is in the process of shifting the balance of power and influence among regional powers. China is emerging as a strong regional and global power. India and Russia also are major powers in the Asia-Pacific. Meanwhile, the US and Japan are facing difficulties in economic growth so their power and role in the region appears to be declining.

In the past 30 years, China's economy has developed rapidly from the 19th to the second biggest economy of the world and is acting as an engine of growth of global economy. China has also become a military power ranking third, after the US and Russia. For the past 20 years, India has had a constant economic growth with a relatively high rate of 6.5 per cent. Indian technologies and defence capabilities have also been developed. India is promoting "Look East Policy" for a more important role and greater influence in the Asia-Pacific. Meanwhile, with advantages of military technology, Russia is looking towards the East for integration and remains a major power in the region and the world.

The shift in power balance has gradually led to emergence of a number of power centres interacting with each other at different levels. The US remains a superpower with the greatest role and influence in the region. US - China relation is the dominant axis of relations to others. Multi-polar order is being formed, which has been seen as the clear feature of the regional power order. This process strongly impacts on regional countries.

US Quadrennial *Defence Review 2010* stated that: *"The United States faces a complex and uncertain security landscape in which the pace of change continues to accelerate. The distribution of global political, economic and military power is becoming more diffuse. The rise of China, the world's most populous country and India, the world's largest democracy, will continue to shape an international system that is no longer easily defined - one in which the United States will remain the most powerful actor but must increasingly work with key allies and partners if it is to sustain stability and peace."*

Cooperation and Competition among Countries

The Asia-Pacific is affected by both globalisation and regionalisation, which are intertwined and have an impact on interdependence among countries in the region. It has encouraged regional countries to work together at both bilateral and multilateral levels to resolve issues of mutual concerns for peace and stability.

Regional cooperation and integration has been shaped and developed. Major entities such as the US, China, Japan, Russia and ASEAN are members of regional mechanisms and fora such as APEC, ARF, ASEAN +, EAS, etc. They are working together on strategic issues of common concern. However, there is competition and rivalry among them for increased role and influence in the regional mechanisms.

The US has strategic interests in the region. The Obama Administration has adjusted policies to strengthen presence in the Asia-Pacific. The economic and financial crisis as well as consequences of wars in Iraq and Afghanistan have caused decline in American strength and power; though, the US continues to be the pre-eminent super-power in the Asia-Pacific and the world. On one hand, the US is trying to build a comprehensive and stable relationship with China. On the other hand, the US and China still have conflicts of interest and influence.

China has increased its role and influence in the region through international trade, investment, economic aid and technical assistance. China has close relations with many ASEAN and regional countries. However; the rise of China not only provides opportunities but also poses challenges to the regional countries. Military modernisation, together with the ever increasing assertive actions in East Sea recently, have increased tensions and concerns in the region.

India continues to promote its "Look East Policy", aiming at creating a stable foothold in Southeast Asia and gradually increasing engagement and influence in East Asia. India is trying to improve its relationship with China but it also competes with China.

Meanwhile, Japan desires to play a more active role in the region, reaffirms its engagement in Southeast Asia by enhancing its presence and influence in Southeast Asia and strives to compete with China for influence in the region.

Peace, Stability and Cooperation: Potential Risks of Instability and Conflicts

Mutual interdependence, intertwined interests and the process of forming a multi-polar world order have promoted regional integration and cooperation for peace and stability. While competing with each other, the U.S, China, India and Russia also have a need to work together to deal with common security challenges. Therefore, the current status of cooperation and competition need to be maintained. Large-scale wars and conflicts are not desirable to maintain and promote peace, security and relative stability in the region.

However, there are potential and unresolved security challenges in the region. Disputes over territory and natural resources on land and at sea are on the rise. In addition, the region faces non-traditional security challenges such as energy security, food security, terrorism, climate change, natural disasters, epidemics, transnational crime; etc.

The disputes over sovereignty of islands and waters in East Asia, especially in the East Sea, are rising and getting more complicated. These disputes not only reflect related parties' stance on territorial sovereignty but also relate to ambition of some countries to control natural resources and geo-strategic areas. Therefore, if involved parties fail to find solutions that reconcile interests of each other and do not respect international laws, especially the 1982 UNCLOS, disputes over islands and waters will not get resolved and potential conflicts are likely to adversely affect security and cooperation in the region.

The East Sea is a very important area in terms of marine resources and international sea lanes. There still exist unresolved sovereignty disputes among claimants. Some countries outside the region also show interests in the East Sea. So far, there have been efforts to resolve the disputes by peaceful negotiations, which has contributed to trust and confidence building and prevention of military clashes. Recently, China and ASEAN have reached an agreement on the Guidelines for the implementation of the 2002 Declaration on the Conduct of Parties in the East Sea (DOC). Recently, at the 18th ASEAN Meeting, ASEAN leaders agreed that they would try to have the DOC signed in the year 2012 on the occasion of the 10th anniversary of the signing of the DOC. However, there are still difficulties and challenges because involved parties have different viewpoints on interpretation of international laws, especially the 1982 UNCLOS and clear identification of disputed areas.

The complex intertwinement of traditional and non-traditional security issues is a challenge to regional peace and stability, which requires regional countries to work together to build effective cooperative frameworks.

Conclusion

Asia - Pacific is one of the most important regions in terms of economic development, international relations and regional integration. Regional geopolitical landscape is having a rapid and complicated change, with opportunities and challenges, cooperation and competition. Peace, stability and development remain mainstreams, but the region also faces numerous complicated traditional and non-traditional challenges. Power balance shift, cooperation and competition between the major powers, as well as the need for cooperation to deal with emerging security challenges, require the region to have an appropriate regional security structure, to ensure an environment of peace, stability and development.

Session I
Third Paper (Seminar Room 1)

Ambassador Andrea Perugini (Italy)

EU Policies on the Asia Pacific Region, including the Asian Subcontinent

In comparison to any other Geopolitical area, Asia Pacific is highly heterogeneous in institutional, economic, cultural, linguistic, religious and civil society terms, comprising highly industrialised and post-industrialised states, large emerging developing states with global ambitions and medium-sized countries with growing ambitious projections and increasing potential as well as less developed countries, still struggling to achieve high rate of growth.

It is, therefore, not possible to take a general systemic approach to the area as a whole. The Asia Pacific requires a methodologically differentiated approach and a flexible set of policy tools. This is a sub continent which is the main driver of growth and of globalisation, but which, at the same time, originates concerns, as such a rise is at the same time perceived as potentially prone to generate hot spots of tension and instability. For these reasons, any approach to a region comprising nearly four billion people and cradle to hundreds of ethnic communities, languages, cultures and traditions must take into account the features of a complex and evolving reality.

Although the EU is not perceived as a full fledged political actor in the Region, the EU and its member states have been involved in the Asia Pacific since 1978 (with ASEAN).

The EU dialogue with the region takes place through a number of instruments: the EU-ASEAN dialogue, a cooperation process which dates back to the end of 1970 and which now involves a wide range of sectors (energy, environment, education, trade, etc,); the ASEM or Asia Europe Meeting, an informal forum for dialogue at political level and a framework for cooperation between Europe and Asia in various spheres (political, economic and cultural, including climate change, energy security, non proliferation, migration, human rights, counter terrorism, labour and employment, economic and financial cooperation); the ASEF (Asia Europe Foundation), the only established institution of ASEM aimed at promoting greater mutual understanding between Asia and Europe through intellectual, cultural and people-to-people exchanges. Finally, ARF (ASEAN Regional Forum), the only regional body to which the EU is party, a forum aimed at promoting regional peace, stability and prosperity in the Asia Pacific Region by fostering dialogue and cooperation on security issues.

The main political strategic objectives of the EU in the Area are as follows:

- Taking part and contributing to the growth process of the continent by encouraging an overall context of stability and regional peace and security, favouring economic integration and social development in a manner which proves sustainable, on the basis of the assumption that the long term security and prosperity of Asia-pacific countries can only be beneficial to stability and economic growth at a global scale.

- Promoting effective multilateralism and cooperating with Asia Pacific countries on all major challenges of a global nature, taking part in the ongoing interaction in the exchange of emerging technologies and their economic benefits (including in the EU-ASEAN, ARF, East Asia Summit and ASEM fora).

- Tackling global threats: energy and food security, poverty, migration, the social dimension of globalisation, overcoming non tariff and trade barriers, facilitating access to raw materials and achieving a more sustainable exploitation, protecting the environment and bio-diversity.

- Contributing to the development of civil societies, based on education, rule of law, tolerance, promoting and protecting human rights, preventing and fighting intolerance and radicalism *vis-a-vis*, religious and ethnic minorities, fostering freedom of belief as a fundamental pillar of a social texture more open to interaction and co-existence between different communities.

- Preventing and stemming nuclear proliferation.

- Supporting dialogue through PCAs and FTAs in order to better exploit the potential added value of a closer interaction and exchange on all fronts between the EU and Asia-Pacific countries.

All the above are based on the assumption in the EU that, in order to preserve its own prosperity and its own security, it must be more outwardly proactive while the opportunities are huge, as are the potential challenges and threats.

The EU needs to better and more fully come to terms with the peaceful rise and the pacific development of major Asian countries and is interested in working at commonly shared objectives in the context of stability, avoiding polarisation or misunderstanding. Global players ought to share global responsibility, a long term view and common benefits. The Asia Pacific region, as it grows, is increasingly *demandeur* of security. Such a demand arises from a majority of Asian countries. Economic, social and political security perceptions are exerting an extraordinary drive to the ongoing regional process of integration in Asia-Pacific. We have made a survey of political and economic regional integration and coordination initiatives in Asia Pacific and we have come up with two full pages of acronyms, which are revealing as to the degree of vitality in the region. But at the same time, they illustrate the fact that the search for direction is still unfolding in the continent; all energies and efforts are converging on one priority: how to make growth sustainable without affecting stability, since there is wide recognition that stability is the most important asset and pre-requisite for growth.

In the EU's view, there are many areas where we seek to increase cooperation with Asia Pacific, in search for a stable and secure architecture.

Let me mention a few: (a) Releasing the full potential of the trade and investment relationship (b) Strengthening the political and security cooperation (in this respect, the EU looks forward to acceding to the ASEAN Treaty of Amity and Cooperation (TAC). (c) Promoting human rights, in particular by working with Asian partners on migration issues, on corporate social responsibility and on human trafficking. (d) The EU is already working with many Asian countries, including in the ASEAN context, in the field of natural disaster preparedness, by sharing knowledge and experience on civilian and military cooperation. (e) The EU is interested in growing cooperation on transnational crime (including people smuggling, drug trafficking, terrorism, cyber crime, border management). (f) The EU follows very closely, issues affecting maritime security and safety and supports attempts to seek a comprehensive approach that focusses on safety of navigation and security concerns. In this respect, the EU could, for instance, support the establishment of a regional mechanism in the Straits of Malacca and Singapore for enhanced maritime safety and marine environment protection. In addition, the Asian continent is host to a number of more localised conflicts which have troubled the region over the years and in several cases, the EU has been able to contribute to relevant confidence-building, conflict-resolution and post-conflict reconstruction activities, drawing on the EU's ability to bring together its political, development and humanitarian instruments. For example, the EU's contribution to the peace process in Aceh, to post conflict development in Timor Leste or more recently, the EU's support for the peace process in Mindanao, have allowed the EU to demonstrate its support for peace and security in the region.

On chemical, biological, radiological and nuclear (CBRN) risk mitigation, the EU is cooperating with third countries in developing institutional capacity, in this area, by creating regional "Centres of Excellence" in order to address risk not only from criminal origin and relating to UNSCR 1540 (proliferation, illicit traffics or sabotage) but also risk from accidental origin (industrial catastrophe, transports of CBRN agents) or from natural origin, such as pandemics.

Intensifying socio-cultural cooperation is also relevant to strengthening the security architecture: 1) involving private sector in dialogue on science, technology and innovation; raising the profile of Europe as a destination for young researchers; raising in general public awareness; 2) mobility of researchers, academicians and students and exchanges between higher education institutions.

Other relevant issues are nuclear energy safety. While the EU is not advocating the use of nuclear energy (in the sense that it is neutral on this topic and leaves such a choice to the sovereign policies of member states), it is nonetheless offering support, purely on safety issues to the countries that have decided to invest in this sector (work is ongoing, for instance, in Vietnam and in the Philippines). As the Fukushima Daiichi nuclear accident demonstrated, the potential trans boundary impact of accidents at nuclear installations requires greater transparency and more action at regional level to promote safety.

The regional security architecture in Asia is becoming exposed to new challenges: territorial disputes, controversies over the principle of freedom of navigation, security and safety at sea, tensions over the survey and exploitation of marine underwater energy resources, threats to the non proliferation regime, growing impact of natural calamities, effects of climate change. Against this backdrop, we are witnessing growing interest in the role of the East Asia Summit, a forum which was created in 2005, comprising the ten ASEAN member states plus India, China, Japan, South Korea, Australia and New Zealand and which expanded itself in 2010 with the admission of Russia and the US. On the one hand, we are aware that there is concern within ASEAN that such an enlargement might affect the so called "centrality of ASEAN"; on the other hand, many ASEAN member states appreciate the benefits of having Russia and the US, in terms of rebalancing of influence among the Asian players, within the Summit. The EU, though already engaged in the ASEM framework, perceives the growing role and relevance of EAS and is looking forward to its closer association with the EAS. This will be the only forum where the EU can interact and have - simultaneously - on Asia Pacific issues, a dialogue with ASEAN, China, Japan, Korea, Australia, NZ, India, Russia and the US. Whereas the EU has a dialogue with the US on Asia Pacific in the framework of the transatlantic dialogue and in the context of NATO, it cannot benefit from any other existing forum such as EAS, where all major global actors discuss Asia Pacific together.

In order to address the changing balance in the Region and the risk of competitive nationalism, the EU is keen on promoting co-operative relations among the key players in East Asia and to encourage all sides to refrain from actions that could be misperceived by others in the Region. There are a number of actions that could be encouraged: promotion of confidence building measures with a view to peaceful and cooperative solutions to disputes over territory and resources; greater transparency on military expenditure, doctrine and institutions; more military to military exchanges both among regional players as well as with EU member states.

All the elements I just illustrated should encourage our Asian partners to fully acknowledge the EU not merely as an economic counterpart, but primarily as a privileged geo strategic and political partner, despite the EU's own institutional specificities and its unique characteristics as a subject of international law which make it so peculiar compared to the US, Russia or China or other major players in the international arena. This is also a result of the Ratification of the Lisbon Treaty in 2010 which allows the EU to have a greater voice and outward projection on global political issues, combining political themes to economic ones on all the wide range of its bilateral relations.

In conclusion and in my capacity as Principal Director for Asia, may I add that these strategic objectives are also relevant, as I believe it was implied in my presentation, to areas of Asia such as the one where we are now, the Subcontinent. As in Asia Pacific, the relevance comes from the extent of global or natural challenges as well as from the demands of the concerned communities. That makes the EU envision specific, regional responses of cooperation including at a broader level, i.e. interregional. In South Asia, the concerted efforts of the EU and the interested countries rely essentially on cooperation agreements. I would like to underline that since 2006, the EU enjoys the status of Observer to the only real regional entity i.e. SAARC.

The complex reality of Pakistan has directed the EU to envision a dialogue involving a broad range of political, economic and security issues. The aim is to build a strategic relationship by forging a partnership for peace and development rooted in shared values, principles and commitments. Respect for human rights, fostering economic and trade links, support to democratic institutions are elements of the EU vision hopefully to be translated into a regular and articulated system of dialogue.

It is with the major country of the Subcontinent, India, that the dialogue with the EU has reached the more intense profile. India and the EU moved into a strategic partnership in 2004. Since then, significant progress was made across the board policy, including the launching of FTA negotiations. The fundamental assumption of pursuing and improving dialogue is that India and the EU share a commitment to democracy and a number of interests on key global challenges and on regional conflicts and security. The potential of India-EU relations as well as EU and the Region is vast and I am convinced that on the EU side, great efforts need to be made in order to demonstrate its role and capacities in the political and security fields.

Session I : Discussion

Issue Raised

China declares that it adheres to a No First Use (NFU) doctrine in terms of its nuclear arsenal, but at the same time it considers a nuclear retaliation to conventional attacks or warnings of such attacks. How convenient is China's NFU?

Responses

(a) The NFU sets down that if China were attacked by either conventional or nuclear forces, it would use nuclear weapons as a last resort. This was laid down almost half a century back. Though the technical advances made since then have renewed the debate, China would still stick to its original policy. The main reason being that the Chinese nuclear stockpile is very small thus determining its behaviour. It would only be used as a last resort. China does not want to give up its NFU doctrine for fear of inciting an arms race. It does not seek to catch up with Russia or the US.

(b) From an Indian perspective, there doesn't seem to be any link between China's NFU and its conventional military build-up. The possession of nuclear stockpile has not stopped them from scaling up their military capabilities.

Issue Raised

The US Department of Defence (DoD) has released a paper on the growing Chinese military capabilities. What is the reaction of both China and the US to it?

Responses

(a) The US DoD report entails a new strategic perception of China.

The Chinese foreign minister has rejected some of the contentions made in the report and with good reason. China is a fast growing power and has every right to spruce up its military capacities. It spends a very small part of its GDP on defence as compared to the US. China today is a free rider on the seas. It depends on the US to ensure freedom of navigation. It seeks to address the situation and assume greater responsibility. On the other hand, the Chinese Government needs to do more to improve transparency. But improving transparency involves mutual understanding. And the way it is understood in China, transparency refers less to media reports and has more to do with the opening of official channels.

(b) China has reacted with hostility to the DoD report and has asked that it not be made public. It has been quick to condemn what it sees as the 'Cold War' mentality of the US and has reservations against US insistence on opening EEZs. They also claim the US missile defence program to be provocative vis-à-vis China, even more than India's. In 2004 in Geneva, China had proposed the banning of all weapons in space, including anti-missile defences, but went ahead to develop some of their own.

(c) The EU too, is concerned about the perception of security and the peaceful rise of China. EU gets the impression that it suits China's purpose to be ambiguous, allows it to pull out of situations easily, without giving explanations. But such a strategy leads to a negative perception of China as a responsible global power, on the world stage. Even in the case of the EU bail out, the perception is that China has been exploiting the current situation of financial crisis. Assuming that China is unaware of the security concerns it triggers off on the path to its overall development does not absolve it of the urgent need to improve transparency. A start could be made by exploring multilateral mechanisms to resolve outstanding issues rather than bilateral approach, which has been characteristic of the Chinese approach. That could help build a better perspective of China's peaceful rise.

Issue Raised

China has been exerting pressure on its borders with India, without provocation. What could be a possible way to address this?

Responses

(a) China has followed a typical pattern of behaviour in its relations with India, also with Japan. It tries to mildly provoke to elicit responses and gauge the willingness and methods of other parties to react. With Japan, this happens on the seas and with India, on land. There is a paucity of perception regarding the locus of the problem. It could be said that China has been trying to unsettle the status quo or alternately, Chinese are trying to set stage for change of status quo by use of force.

(b) Chinese actions on the ground go against the estimates of the last speaker. China tries hard to keep status quo. With India, it has signed two treaties to encourage CBMs and peaceful solution to the border dispute, first in 1993 and then 1996. This mechanism has worked well for almost two decades. Vis-à-vis India, China is already in the lead and has no incentive to disturb the status quo. At the 10th Party Congress in 2002, it was even resolved that China would maintain the status quo for at least another 20 years.

Issue Raised

What is China's present policy vis-à-vis the border dispute with India?

Response

China believes that before a final settlement is reached, the status quo should be maintained. There exists a very good mechanism of special representatives. Both sides are keen for an early settlement of the issue. But it is an old issue involving historical legacies on both sides. Thus one feels that an appropriate solution is more important than an early solution.

STRATEGIC AND SECURITY ENVIRONMENT IN THE REGION

As of now, the status quo holds good for both parties.

Issue Raised

The situation of stalemate regarding the nuclearisation of North Korea and Iran is a major cause of concern. China, the US, or the International community seems unable to stem the development. How does China envisage the situation?

Responses

(a) China stands strongly against nuclear proliferation. It is deeply involved with the situation in North Korea. Being a neighbour, it affects Chinese interests more than Iran. The US and South Korea have been insisting that North Korea give up its weaponisation program before coming to the negotiating table and North Korea is opposed to that, resulting in a stalemate. Here China seeks to play the role of an effective mediator. It is in close contact with South Korea and hopes to make the six party talks bear results. In the future, if talks fail, China might explore options with South Korea as well as North Korea. It is strongly against turbulence in the region.

(b) Iran is a signatory to the NPT and as such, China strongly opposes its nuclear program. However, in light of the current evidence of their possible weaponisation, China thinks it is unwise to use force. Such actions would lead to enormous turbulence in the region and affect peace and stability, the world over.

Issue Raised

Currently, in the Asia Pacific region, the high seas are like highways - devoid of any rules. Should there be a maritime legal consensus for the region as a prerequisite to address the various disputes on the seas?

Responses

(a) In the maritime domain, the ANGLOS does set out some basic rules, however, its interpretation differs across actors. The situation in South China sea is rapidly changing with countries like Vietnam and Philippines openly standing behind the right to freedom of navigation. However, the notion of a region-specific set of rules is misleading. Any norm developed for the seas should be global and inclusive.

(b) China is supportive of multilateral engagements for the resolution of disputes and global norms of engagement. However, in the case of the South China Sea, it has been sticking to bilateral negotiations, as it feels this is more suited to the issue at hand.

Issue Raised

What are the factors that could possibly lead some of the countries in the Asia Pacific region to go nuclear? What mechanisms could be developed to guarantee security of the region then?

Response

It is not difficult to envisage a point where the US will have decreased will to enforce treaty obligations and countries like South Korea, Japan and Vietnam will decrease their reliance on US military protection. Japan is already a para-nuclear State with vast holdings of fissile material. Shinzo Abe in 2010 declared, that 'what is in India's interest is in Japan's interest', pointing towards existing doubts on the reliability on the US as a security guarantor. Taiwan too openly talks about its Tai-Ching project. While South Korea has overtly given up nuclearisation, whether the US will come to the rescue of these states in the future is the central question. The economic decline of the US provides some clues. Therefore, one could foresee a retreat of the US from the Asia Pacific region, giving way to Chinese influence.

Issue Raised

Taiwan seems to be covertly turning into a nuclear power. What is the Chinese strategy concerning Taiwan?

Response

China-Taiwan relations have improved in the past half a decade, to the benefit of both parties. Future prospects of political collaboration remain uncertain, but immense scope for cooperation exists. China believes that the future of Taiwan should be determined by Taiwanese people.

Issue Raised

What are the specific military concerns of the US, regarding China? Does the development of a sea-air battle strategy betray concerns of Chinese attack?

Responses

(a) The US is keener to engage China rather than the other way around. It is also more favourable towards the inclusion of Japan and India on the UNSC with veto powers, something that China opposes. As for changing battle strategy, air sea formations merely mean joint work of air force and the navy. The US government has specifically denied that it is directed by concerns against the Chinese.

(b) On the Chinese side, the media and the government have played down their growing expertise in air-sea battle. It is generally believed in China that overconfidence causes war. Thus the claim is that the new strategy is designed to protect assets inside China.

Issue Raised

How will reduction in the defence budget of the US affect its security policies in the Asia Pacific region?

Response

The US is committed to not just stay engaged, but to play a leading role in the region. It is unlikely to abandon Asia anytime soon.

Issues Raised

What role do the EU and Russia see for themselves in a security architecture in the Asia-Pacific? There had been some talk of playing a balancing role through the East Asia Summit (EAS) forum. What specifically do these actors understand by balancing?

Responses

(a) For the EU, balancing would involve looking for equilibrium in the area, with the awareness that China, Japan, India and Russia are interested equally in the emergence of a multi-polar situation, with adequate checks and balances. The EAS could be a forum to realise this. The problem of the EU is that it is not yet sufficiently cohesive to act as a unitary state.

(b) Russia is a relatively new player in this region. Since the fall of the Soviet Union; till very recently, Russia focussed primarily on the West, to prove that it is still an important actor. It has only been a year that Russia has started to seriously look at Asia and seek a role. It is not an easy task, as Russia is not seen as an integral part of the Asian environment, despite the fact that most of its territory lies in Asia. For Russia, balancing refers to the balancing of growing Chinese economic influence. Russia also fears being used as a bargaining chip in a hypothetical future escalation of tensions between the US and China. Russia wants to be independent and would like to keep its hands free. It also recognises that vis-à-vis China and US, Russia is the weaker power. Russia is also deeply concerned over the North Korean issue. While North Korea looks to China with respect, dependence and fear, it is not as mindful of Russia. Russia proposed some changes for the North Korean settlement, involving economic and energy components but that was not considered seriously.

(c) India too needs to spruce up its engagement with the Asia Pacific and for that it needs to substantiate its Look East policy thrust and possibly go beyond.

Session I
Chairman's Concluding Remarks

Shri SK Bhutani, IFS (Retd)

It is my duty reluctantly to bring this discussion to an end. I request you to please join me in thanking the panel for being patient with the questions, giving candid answers and helping the cause of transparency in our dealings.

SESSION II

EXISTING POLITICAL AND ECONOMIC FRAMEWORKS IN THE ASIA PACIFIC-HAVE THEY FULFILLED REGIONAL ASPIRATIONS?

Auditorium

Chairman	-	Rear Admiral Sumihiko Kawamura, Okazaki Institute, Japan.
First Paper	-	Dr Man-Jung Mignonne Chan, Prospect Foundation, Taiwan.
Second Paper	-	Lieutenant General PC Katoch, PVSM, UYSM, AVSM, SC (Retd).
Third Paper	-	Sr Col Vu Van Khanh, IDS, Vietnam.

Seminar Room 1

Chairman	-	Professor Richard Rigby, ANU, Australia.
First Paper	-	Mr Hideki Asari, JIIA, Japan.
Second Paper	-	Professor Moon Jangnyeol, RINSA, South Korea.
Third Paper	-	Dr Claudia Astarita, CeMiSS, Italy.

Discussion (In Auditorium)

Session II (Auditorium)
Chairman's Opening Remarks

Rear Admiral Sumihiko Kawamura (Japan)

We have gathered here to examine the topic of "Existing Political and Economic Frameworks in the Asia-Pacific - Have They Fulfilled Regional Aspirations"? We have presentations by three distinguished speakers, namely Dr Mignonne Man-Jung Chan from Taiwan, Lt Gen PC Katoch from India and Sr Col Vu Van Khanh from Vietnam. I can say from twenty years experience as defence analyst or active participant in international forums that for all the well written and meaningful papers by panelists, the presentations have a tendency to take longer. Thus my job today is mostly of a time keeper. Each presenter has twenty minutes, to be followed by joint discussion afterwards. I expect your cooperation and understanding. First coming up is Dr Mignonne Man-Jung Chan.

Session II

First Paper (Auditorium)

Dr Mignonne Man-Jung Chang (Taiwan)

Asia-Pacific and Regional Integration: Geo-economic and Geo-strategic Challenges

The paper is in five parts as under :-

- Shifting Geo-economic landscape,
- Regional Integration- 'Competitive liberalisation or same bed-different dreams?'
- Sino-US relations – Myth or Reality of G2
- Taiwan's roles in regional integration
- Possible dream of mind-body-soul trilogy?

Shifting Geo-economic Landscape

The fortunes of the powerful, the resurged and the emerging players seem to be rapidly changing. This is evident from the sinking of the US and Europe. While in the former the Lehman-Brothers crisis triggered off a movement that led to the downgrading of its credit ratings from AAA to AA+ (by the S&P), Europe continues to struggle with a Sovereign Wealth Fund crisis and rescue packages for the crippled economies of Portugal, Greece, Ireland and Spain. Joseph Stiglitz mentioned that America and Europe are 'marching alone towards the declaration of a grand debacle' and warned of the contagious effects of political bickering and debatable policies such as Keynesian stimulus that fuelled deeper recession and higher budget deficits. He also said that massive spending cuts in the US and austerity programs in Europe could lead to unacceptably high levels of unemployment, possibly for years.

On the other hand, China has been resurging at a furious pace, leading to doubts over whether such rise would be assertive or constructive. There is also a considerable power shift, with China, a leading force in the BRIC, BRICS and now possibly the CIVITS.

China is also looking at Asian emerging markets as key export destinations. With the rates of inflation in the big emerging markets swelling (as of 2011 it remained at 8.6 per cent in India, 5.8 per cent in Indonesia and 4.1 per cent in South Korea), the Chinese involvement in the G2 and the benefits it brings for the countries of the Asia Pacific remain to be seen.

Regional Integration: 'Competitive Liberalisation or Same Bed-Different Dreams?'

If integration is understood as a sequence of development beginning from a customs union, common market union, economic union and then political union, the EU lies economically united and close to complete political union, while the ASEAN and other Free Trade Agreements in the area are still at the first few stages. The initial attempts at regional integration in the Asia Pacific were driven solely by the ASEAN. Its strategic goal setting envisaged the achievement of peace, security and economic prosperity through equal emphasis on cultural understanding, political security and economic integration.

The region witnesses two large multilateral mechanisms the ASEAN and the APEC, in a scenario of competitive liberalisation. While the ASEAN is the driving force behind the Intra ASEAN, ASEAN + 1, ASEAN + 3, ASEAN + 6 and EAS moves, the APEC has been the driving force behind the Bogor Goal, the REI, the FTAAP and the TPP. While the frameworks for political and security issues are taken up regularly in the CSCAP, the ASEAN Regional Forum and the EAS, which one evolves as the bed rock of regional integration remains to be seen.

Sino-US Relations: Myth or Reality of G2

Currently, the Sino-US bilateral relations are the most important in the world.

They hold strategic and economic dialogues twice a year. Therein the key issues of discussion are climate change and energy security, the global economy, the US trade deficit and the weak dollar and military cooperation. The last envelops crucial issues like the nuclearisation of North Korea and Iran, the issue of sales of arms to Taiwan and concerns of human rights

As for China, the PRC has been characteristically ambivalent regarding its military build-up. Is it for peaceful rise, as is often promised? The Pentagon report to the US Congress in 2011 stated that as of 2009, the PRC had 1,000 short range missiles opposite Taiwan and was upgrading the lethality of this force. China is also said to have the world's most active land based ballistic and cruise missile program and is rapidly modernising its nuclear forces. The PLA's navy also has the largest fleet of fighting ships in Asia, with more than 60 submarines, 55 medium and large amphibious vessels and roughly 85 missile-equipped patrol crafts. Its ground forces are 1.25 million in strength with a third of it stationed in three military regions opposite Taiwan.

Moreover, its declarations on peaceful military development need to be taken with a pinch of salt, considering recent actions. These involve decoupling effects in regional emerging economies from dependence on the US to China, bringing with it constant spates over unfair trade, currency manipulation and the outward movements of Sovereign Wealth Funds. Added to this are regional spotlights on cyber security, overlapping of territorial claims and disputes, maritime disputes and navy exercises. The cases of Senkaku Islands and the South China Sea dispute, especially, have the potential to snowball into confrontation.

Under such circumstances, the scenarios for regional geopolitical environment are-US and China both exercise their soft power; US exercises hard power and China soft power; US exercises soft power and China hard power; both exercise hard power. As of 2011, the US looked to play an increasingly important role in Asia. Indeed Hillary Clinton had declared that US looked to not only engage with, but to lead Asia. Its APEC slogan for the year was 'To get the stuff done'. With China typically reluctance to be self assertive and assume greater role in world affairs, it remains to be seen whether the G2 emerges as a trick or treat for the Asia Pacific Region.

Taiwan's Role in the Region

The changing trade portfolio brought by ASEAN + China has had negative economic impact on Taiwan. Increasing cross straits trade has been seen to lead to growing trade surpluses and Taiwan hopes to address this disparity through negotiations of ECFA. For Taiwan to springboard to global competitiveness, it would need not being marginalised while building FTA's, with other like minded partners, to forge strategic alliances to create win-win partnerships, to collaborate joint development projects in regional and global organisations.

In the region, Taiwan is committed unilaterally to peace and prosperity. This is pursued through bilateral trade agreements. The ECFA is engaged as an engine of growth, a catalyst to regional integration and model of conflict resolution. Taiwan and Singapore are also likely to start ASTEP negotiations and sign investment agreements with Japan. It also looks at the ECFA as a catalyst for Taiwan and South Korea cooperation. Finally, it has been engaged in multi-lateral participation in the region for human security. Some of the measures taken are towards emergency preparedness, aviation safety, climate change, proliferation security initiatives and cyber security.

Taiwan's initiative in the APEC has spanned across the APEC digital opportunity centre, the one village one product initiative, SME risk management centre, APEC Typhoon centre and in the making of the APEC Green Building.

A Possible Dream of Body-Mind-Soul Trilogy?

In keeping with the goal of building a enduring security architecture in the Asia-Pacific Region, I propose a model, a possible dream of body-mind-soul trilogy. The body herein is envisaged as the institutional arrangement operating in the region. Mind is understood as the action of goal setting, modus operandi and initiatives. Most immediate examples are the Bogor goals, OAA, concerted unilateralism/ critical mass/ path finder or APEC X and EVSL, ITC, ITCII and EGS. Soul would then be understood as balanced approach to non-zero sum game. It would involve flexible, voluntary and non-binding approaches, the acceptance of different paces of change, focus on mutual respect and mutual benefit and attempts to manage crises from the same boat. One hopes that such a framework would contribute towards a lasting period of peace, stability and prosperity in the region.

Session II
Second Paper (Auditorium)

Lieutenant General PC Katoch, PVSM, UYSM, AVM, SC (Retd)

Existing Political and Economic Frameworks in the Asia-Pacific- Have they fulfilled Regional Aspirations?

Asia-Pacific is a dynamic region encompassing numerous countries, including Australia and New Zealand in the South and its locus in ASEAN, offers tremendous opportunities for global exporters. In a world where bulk consumers in most countries reside outside own borders, APEC itself comprises 40 per cent of the global population. Many of these dynamic economies are growing faster than the world average and together generated 56 per cent of global GDP in 2010. While the ASEAN sponsored AFTA (Asian Free Trade Area) is gaining momentum, the EAS (East Asia Summit) too has been focussing on issues of trade, energy and security. Then there are non-traditional security issues that affect the well-being, dignity and the very survival of human beings, which are beyond the confines of state sovereignty and territorial integrity. These need to be addressed. The future success of the Asia Pacific Region will depend on its further global integration with the world becoming flatter in every aspect including economic and physical well being and security.

Cooperation in the Asia Pacific Region is being overshadowed with mounting strife in the South China Sea and the lack of appropriate regional security arrangement, notwithstanding the 2020 Vision Statement of the ARF, recognising ARF as a central pillar in the emerging regional security architecture and efforts by the EAS (East Asia Summit). Moreover, with world seaborne trade pegged to reach 41,800 billion tonne miles by 2014, with half the world's super tanker traffic passing through the region's waters and lack of a multilateral approach that has failed to combat maritime security challenges holistically, strife and conflict are likely to heighten in the Asia Pacific region.

Region and Groupings

Asia itself is a volatile region with large standing armies, four declared nuclear weapon states, states that are engaged in production and export of missiles, besides having seven of the 10 most populous countries of the world. Its demography, civilization and political diversity provide additional volatility. It has been estimated that in the next 25 years, Asia will account for 57 per cent of world's GDP. That is why the 21st Century is being referred to as the "Asian Century" albeit recession in the West will keep affecting this region. The management of unpredictable behaviour of the economy is also coupled with security implications that plague this region. South East Asia has historically been an area of great geostrategic significance for centuries. It derives its geostrategic significance by virtue of its location of sitting astride the waters that connect the Indian Ocean with the Pacific Ocean and the strategic chokepoints of the Malacca Straits, the Lombok Straits and the Sunda Straits. The sea-lanes traversing the South East region carry 50 per cent of the global trade and 33 per cent of the world's oil. More than 550 million people inhabit South East Asia and the regional economies total upwards of US $ 1 trillion. The economies of the United States and those of US allies like Japan, South Korea, Philippines, Taiwan and Australia heavily depend on stability in South East Asia and more specifically, the security of sea-lanes on which depends their trade, commerce and energy security. 97 per cent of Indian trade is by sea and the US$ 60 billion annual China-India trade is also primarily by sea. In Asia, some major sub-regional groups are ASEAN, SAARC and cross-sub-regional blocs are ASEAN Free Trade Area (APTA), APEC, BIMSTEC, etc. Bilateral trade pacts are also being pursued for deep integration. Sub-regions are also building up network with other countries and regions separately, for example, ASEAN+3, ASEAN+6, ASEAN-China, ASEAN-India. Though trade is the main vehicle of cooperation, other areas are also included in the cooperation activities.

ASEAN, established in 1967 as a geo-political and economic

organisation of 10 countries of Southeast Asia has expanded over the years. ASEAN aims at accelerated economic growth, social progress, cultural development, protection of regional peace and stability and a forum for discussing differences. Post the East Asian Financial Crisis of 1997, there has been better integration between the economies of ASEAN as well as the ASEAN +3 countries (China, Japan and South Korea). Aside from improving each member state's economies, the bloc has also focussed on peace and stability in the region, ratifying the Southeast Asian Nuclear-Weapon-Free-Zone Treaty.

The idea of East Asia Groupings, mooted in 1995, has resulted in a number of EAS (East Asia Summits) involving ASEAN + 3 countries (China, Japan and ROK) as well as countries that are Full Dialogue Partner status of ASEAN and Accession to the Treaty of Amity and Cooperation (TAC). The EAS focusses on multiple issues like energy, finance, education, avian flu, closer coordination among the national emergency response and management mechanisms for natural disaster mitigation, environment, climate change, sustainable development and mutual appreciation of each other's heritage and history, leading to initiatives like revival of Nalanda University in India, plus a Track Two study on a Comprehensive Economic Partnership in East Asia (CEPEA) and establishment of an Economic Research Institute for ASEAN and East Asia (ERIA). Adoption of the "Singapore Declaration on Climate Change, Energy and Environment" led to mobilising financial support, capacity building, development of clean technologies, exchange of scientific and technical expertise, joint studies, promotion of public awareness and development of policy measures.

China is playing an important role in South East Asia with its development interest as the driving force and is making strategic inroads in South Asia as well. The People's Republic of China (PRC) has performed very well in South East Asia on the economic front. It has been particularly successful in establishing close trade ties with ASEAN. The China-ASEAN free trade agreement signed in 2010 is well known, as is its participation in a lot of sub-regional cooperation arrangements. ASEAN-India cooperation covers numerous fields like trade and investment, science and technology (including

IT, biotechnology, advanced materials, space sciences and their applications), tourism, human resource development, education, including language training, transport, infrastructure, health and pharmaceuticals. A Joint Declaration on Cooperation to Combat International Terrorism has been made and India is a signatory to the Treaty of Amity and Cooperation in Southeast Asia. An ASEAN India Media Exchange Program has been established. The India-ASEAN Trade-in-Goods Agreement came into force in January, 2010. The India-ASEAN Commemorative Summit is planned in 2012 where the India-ASEAN Vision 2020 document would also be unveiled, taking into account the shift in global economy towards Asia. This summit is likely to lead to new initiatives and see an exchange of ideas on global and regional issues.

India has also achieved progress in improving intra-ASEAN connectivity as well as connectivity with its dialogue partners. There are over 215 direct and indirect flights every week between India and Singapore, 115 flights with Thailand and 50 with Malaysia. The work on the Trilateral Highway Project between India, Myanmar and Thailand is progressing. ASEAN-India also proposed, in 2010, to build a new highway connecting India-Myanmar-Laos-Cambodia-Vietnam. Similarly, under the Mekong-Ganga Cooperation program, an agreement has been reached to build Delhi-Hanoi rail link. Under ICT connectivity Optical Fibres have been laid upto Mandalay in Myanmar. An Open Skies Agreement (OSA) is being formalised through Joint Working Groups. Under ASEAN-India economic cooperation there are more than 40 projects under various stages of execution, including Collaborative R&D and Workshop on Thermally Sprayed Ceramic-based Coatings, establishment of a Digital S&T Library in ASEAN countries, Human Resource Development in Free and Open Source Software, establishing VSAT based Tele-Education and Tele-medicine network in countries, training of ASEAN Diplomats in India Establishment of Centres of English Language Training (CELT) and Entrepreneurship Development Centres (EDC).

Trade and Free Trade

The rise of China and India is being analysed in various forums. Building a regional architecture and institutions that will sustain growth and deepen international integration while also managing accompanying risks of economic or political instability on global systems is a major priority. Measured in purchasing power parity (PPP) terms, Asia's share of global GDP will amount to around 31 per cent in 2020, of which China alone will account for over 14 percentage points. These projections suggest that China and India will have substantial impact on the world economy. The case for using PPP data rather than initial market exchange rate data to project future structure of world output rests on the likelihood that substantial exchange rate appreciations in rapidly growing economies (such as China) will more accurately reflect their weight in the world economy in coming years. The scale and weight of income growth in Asia will have a huge impact on trade in goods and services, both globally and within the region. The income growth projected cannot be sustained without continuing to maintain the openness to international trade and private capital flows that has helped to drive successful growth in the past. Increased incomes in the Asian economy will lift the importance of Asian trade in world trade. Asian share in every country's international trade will grow, on average, commensurately with Asia's growth in world trade share. For some economic partners, such as Asian economies and Australia, proximity to the region and complementary economic and trade structures will intensify intra-regional trade and investment ties as Asia experiences deeper integration with global markets.

South Asian global trade is estimated to be at a level that is less than half its potential, given the scale and structure of the economy. East Asia, including China, is closer to achieving its trade potential than South Asia. However, national and global efforts can also be assisted by regional cooperation. Trade is an engine of driver in ASEAN and East Asia, but South Asia still has to cover more distance. Even within ASEAN, divergent views are quite common for further integration, mainly with China and India. Presently, every state has enormous autonomy over trade matters including from taxes to procedures. Through unilateral liberalisation process, many of the Asian economies achieved high growth. Due to diverse nature of economies, integration process through economic cooperation has become complicated and slow. That does not imply that Asian economies need to wait for further convergence. Initial conditions are important but not decisive for integration.

Since its establishment in 1989, APEC has facilitated growth of participants by optimising interdependence among Asia-Pacific economies and to enhance a sense of community. It aims to improve regional trade and economic performance and linkages for the prosperity of the people in the region. It has helped to reduce tariffs and other barriers to trade across the Asia-Pacific region. Business transaction costs have been reduced considerably (around 10 per cent). It has worked to create an environment to ensure the safe and efficient movement of goods, services and people across borders through policy decisions and economic and technical cooperation. APEC member economies have grown and developing economies in particular have experienced increases in GDP and standards of living. In 2010, APEC put forward its agenda with the theme "Change and Action", key priorities being regional economic integration, development of the Growth Strategy and human security - to further develop and integrate the Asia-Pacific region in the 21st century, moving towards an economically-integrated, robust and secure APEC community. APEC 2011 focusses on realising the 2010 vision, in pursuit of APEC's central mission of promoting trade and investment in order to increase economic growth and employment in the Asia-Pacific, building towards a seamless regional economy that will ensure long-term prosperity in the region by achieving practical, concrete and ambitious results.

FTAs (Free Trade Areas) enable free internal trade while external tariffs against outside countries differ among member nations. These factors create the "trade creation effect" and the "trade diversion effect" through respective actions of a shift in the geographic location of production from higher-cost to lower-cost member nations as well as a shift in the locus of production of formerly imported goods from lower-cost non-member nations to higher-cost member nations. The FTA is thought to stimulate intra-area trade and obstruct extra-area trade through these two static effects. By the same analogy, AFTA (ASEAN Free Trade Area) enables countries to move outside their erstwhile production possibilities and secures capital as well as consumption goods from other parts of the world. However, free trade can result in unemployment in industries that are comparatively disadvantageous. This effect arises in every trading country, at least in the short term, necessitating certain institutions to rearrange unemployed workers, state's marketing policy, vocational training and the like. More importantly, any initial condition of unequal endowments like physical capital, scientific capacities, entrepreneurial abilities, capacity to carry out technological research is likely to be exacerbated by free trade. The negative effects of this cumulative process are greater for less developed countries than for developed countries.

Security

During the Cold War, South East Asia region witnessed power-play between the US and the Soviet Union. Both maintained naval bases in the region with their naval fleets patrolling the high seas. China was a marginal player then. However, with the rise of China, especially on the territorial and resources fronts, Chinese policies are giving rise to conflict with her neighbours. Economic prowess of China is supported by massive foreign direct investment (around US$ 106 billion in 2010 alone) which is a catalyst to growth. As much as China may portray her peaceful intentions and say that her interests are purely economic, her territorial assertiveness and past record does not instill much confidence, which is likely to increase conflict in the region directly affecting regional cooperation, economic and political security. A cross section believes that this Chinese mindset is well-rooted in her historical "Tian Xia" (Under the Heaven) Concept which views "all territories" as belonging to the Chinese and due to which, the Chinese, traditionally, attach no sense to territory.

Additionally, due to Chinese aspirations to emerge as the second pole in a new global strategic order, the South East Asia region is increasingly emerging as the arena for strategic power-play and tussle between China and the United States. While there is a general expectation in Southeast Asia to have the US as a security guarantor in order to counter the rising Chinese influence, certain regional powers are ambivalent on the issue. Their economic and trade dependence on China could be a reason for the same. There seems to be no sound mechanism in Southeast Asia to deal with issues like Thailand-Cambodia border problem or the Malaysia-Indonesia sea boundary. China's claim to entire South China Sea, Spratly and Paracel group of islands has aggravated tensions. The South East Asian countries embarked on a spree of arms purchases after mid-2000s with a focus on building up their naval, submarine and fighter jets assets to upgrade their defensive capabilities, in order to withstand any aggressive instincts and strategic coercion by China. In the coming years, one can expect that the South East Asia region emerges as a hotly contested region strategically between the US and China. There are fundamental positional differences between the US and China, which affect the strategic situation in South East Asia. The US stand that the case of the disputed Senkaku Island comes under the jurisdiction of US-Japan security treaty is considered as a serious challenge by Beijing. A second example is the US contention that the South China Sea islands dispute should be solved by multilateral efforts. China strongly opposes the same with its counter point that the issue should be solved bilaterally.

China, as a major power in Asia to reckon with, has historically viewed the South East Asian region as its strategic backyard and wants the US, as an interloper, to quit the region. China has declared South China Sea as her Core Concern which implies that China is prepared to go to war even to ensure this declared sovereignty. The US, along with other nations, has declared that the Global Commons, which do not get limited only to maritime waters but extend to air-space and outer space are the common heritage of everyone as they provide the connective tissue for communications and no single state can declare sovereignty over them. During the ARF meet in July 2010, Hillary Clinton had stated that US "has a national interest in freedom of navigation, open access to Asia's maritime commons and respect for international law in the South China Sea". Appraisal of intentions of the US and China in the region, indicates towards strategic confrontation between the two in the 21st Century, particularly in the South East Asian region. However much China would like to see the exit of the US from South East Asia strategically, this is unlikely to take place. On the contrary, the US seems to be intent on getting embedded deeper in South East Asia. While China may not have enough leg-space to achieve its end strategic aims in South East Asia in relation to the US, it is unlikely to give up and therein exist the portents of a long drawn out strategic confrontation.

A Vision Statement for ARF (ASEAN Regional Forum) for 2020 was adopted at the 16th ARF Ministerial in July 2009. It recognised ARF as the central pillar in the emerging regional security architecture, calling for strengthening ARF's role in raising awareness on security challenges and intensifying confidence building and cooperation. A Plan of Action (POA) for implementation of the Vision Statement was adopted in July 2010. The POA contains policy guidance for the Forum to develop and implement concrete and practical actions including in the fields of disaster relief, maritime security, non-proliferation and disarmament, counter-terrorism and peacekeeping. The POA recommends that by 2020, ARF should continue its efforts on consolidating CBMs. It also suggests measures for expanding and enhancing the effectiveness of ARF's institutional features. The 18th ARF Ministerial, held on 23 July 2011, adopted a Work Plan on Preventive Diplomacy as well as a Work Plan on Maritime Security, which provides the framework for taking forward cooperation activities, in respective areas.

The Present

There is no denying the fact that the Asia Pacific Region is economically stronger than what it was a decade plus back and has managed to get over the 1997 recession comfortably. However, the increase in individual GDPs includes the profits made by the MNCs. The rapidity with which ASEM member countries have opened their economies in the last few years is impressive. Although all of the Southeast Asian economies initially embarked on import-substituting industrialisation, over time they shifted to export-oriented industrialisation policies. Export-oriented industrialisation led to an opening of the economies to more markets and the promotion of foreign direct investment (FDI) as a means of upgrading the industrial structures through the transfer and diffusion of advanced industrial technologies. As a result, the exposure of the economies to foreign trade became large. While most Asian countries reduced their dependence on US and EU, China has increased its share to these markets. Movements in both trade volumes and world market prices for traded commodities have impacted on the foreign demand for ASEM country exports in various degrees. The importance of foreign firms in the export sector is well-documented and there is ample evidence that export orientation is one of the most important determinants of FDI flows. The current downturn in economic activity throughout Asia highlights the vulnerability of the export-led economic growth model to external shocks. This situation has engendered widespread interest in a rebalancing of the economies in a way that would shift export-driven growth to domestic demand-led growth. The fundamental question facing policymakers is how to rebalance growth in a manner that reduces the region's external market dependence without negatively impacting on their economies during the transition process.

Trade is a major driver in ASEAN and East Asia, but South Asia appears to be going slow. Even within ASEAN, there are divergent views for further integration. As things stand, every state has enormous autonomy over trade matters right from taxes to procedures. Through the unilateral liberalisation process, many of the Asian economies achieved high growth. Due to diverse nature of economies, the integration process through economic cooperation has become complicated and slow. That does not imply that Asian economies need to wait for further convergence. Initial conditions are important but not decisive for integration. At the same time, less developed countries that have large pools of unskilled labour and use this force intensively for products that may be good for trade, have the danger of locking themselves into a stagnant situation inhibiting the domestic growth of elements of capital, entrepreneurship, technical skills and the like, which are indispensable for future development. Static efficiency can thus become long term dynamic inefficiency, which is detrimental to holistic growth. Growth, therefore, can be lopsided. Trade and commerce apart, upgrading human resources, living standards, environment, conservation, poverty mitigation are issues that require constant focus.

The role of MNCs (Multi National Corporations) also needs to be examined dispassionately notwithstanding their contribution to development. MNCs, which are an omnipresent reality, need to be taken into account in analysing the impact of FTA on ASEAN development and the Asia Pacific region as a whole. Because of MNCs' penetration in deregulated areas, FTAs may increase the risk of negative effects. With proliferation of MNCs and their increasing foreign ownership, low income strata population of less developed countries may not benefit at all from these exports. MNCs divert resources away from food production toward the manufacture of sophisticated products that primarily cater to the demands of local elites and foreign consumers. They also tend to exacerbate the imbalance between rural and urban economic opportunities by concentrating primarily in urban export enclaves in projects not conducive to holistic social growth, thus contributing to excessive rural-urban migration.

Future

Though Asia Pacific region countries have their own individual sovereignties, a future environment of closer cooperation should aim for the following:-

- Help develop less developed countries by enabling them (as a group) to receive favourable trade concessions from developed countries, especially in the form of the lowered barriers for their exports of labour-intensive manufactured goods, plus permitting creation of "regional trading blocs" among developing countries at relatively equal stages of industrial development and similar market sizes. This kind of "regional trading bloc" similar to the EU may offer better prospects for balanced and diversified development.

- Measures should be adopted to avoid resources being allocated to socially undesirable projects and encourage MNC participation on basis of holistic growth. Unchecked MNC participation can lead to distortion of the socio-economic structure of ASEAN countries.

- ASEAN countries must expand the actual AFTA to a wider global economic zone and encompass the entire Asia Pacific region as a first step.

- The position of AFTA within the East Asian economies should not diminish the independence of ASEAN countries, subordinating them to the stronger countries. Every country must be able to equally benefit from the regional trading bloc of developing countries at relatively equal stages of industrial development with an enlarged AFTA.

- ASEAN and AFTA need to acknowledge that strong member countries of the WTO do not desire total liberalisation, but only a liberalisation which favours individual national interests. This has been demonstrated time and again. To that end, ASEAN-WTO relations need to be treated with caution. Additionally, under the FTA, which assures a total liberalised area, no institutions can regulate or control the activities of MNCs. In this sense, the FTA must not be considered an extension of the actual WTO, but should be seen as a strong step towards concretising the MNCs' dream.

- To ensure public participation in development, Track III dialogue in ASEAN and Asia Pacific region needs to be given due weightage, especially since Track I represents governments and Track II, generally, government sponsored think tanks. This will ensure better and holistic growth, taking into account grass root issues. Empowering communities should be part of the development process.

- Issues like resource management, climate change, energy and environmental security, nuclear and missile proliferation, disarmament, poverty alleviation, counter terrorism and transnational crime need more focus. There is a need to have an overarching structure to tackle these challenges. Current Asia Pacific regional arrangements also fail to effectively separate political, economic and security issues which lead to an organisation like APEC to also tackle non-traditional security issues, apart from its main remit of economic cooperation.

- The ASEAN-China free trade pact provides more advantageous terms to the regional nations than what India's recently signed similar pact does. The "services" sector is still outside the purview of India-ASEAN FTA; an anomaly that needs to be corrected. Also, India can offer assistance to East Asian nations in building capabilities to protect the sea lanes of communication. There is also tremendous scope for India's cooperation with Southeast Asian nations in the non-traditional security field.

- Energy policy and technology lead to a slowdown in the growth of CO_2 emissions from energy use – but not fast enough to put the world on a safe carbon trajectory. Global emissions growth is likely to decelerate annually from 1.9 per cent in 1990-2010 to 1.2 per cent for period 2010-30; OECD emissions are likely to be lower in 2030 than 2010, but this decline is more than offset by the growth in non OECD emissions. More aggressive policies could see CO_2 emissions from energy use, starting to fall after 2020, with richer countries cutting emissions and developing countries more likely to reduce carbon intensity. Globally, the greatest scope for emission reduction remains in power generation. Asia Pacific should keep this focus.

- Improvement in Asian integration process can be further improved in the evolving convergence mechanism among various groups. A cue can be taken from the structure of BIMSTEC which focusses on the micro issues like sectoral cooperation apart from macro issues like trade agreements. This idea can develop another layer of cooperation which can reassure the integration process.

- Non-traditional security issues affect the well-being, dignity and the very survival of human beings which are beyond the confines of state sovereignty and territorial integrity. The response to these threats, therefore, would have to be cooperative and inter-state because national responses, in all probability, will be inadequate.

- Finally, the region has the potential for conflict, as mentioned above. The ARF has a major role to play in this regard, including promoting peaceful discussion on territorial gains, maritime disputes and protection of sea lanes of communications. It needs no emphasis to say that conflict, chances of which are high, will retard progress in the Asia Pacific region. Dialogue could take a cue from CICA (Conference on Interaction and Confidence Building Measures in Asia) aimed at enhancing cooperation, through elaborating multilateral approaches towards promoting peace, security and stability. The question of resolving or at least managing the regional security environment has become more important as calls for an effective security arrangement are being made in response to the changing dynamics which affects Asia Pacific stability. Various security challenges brought about by the rise of China, the growing recognition of the impact of transnational and non-traditional security concerns, along with traditional security concerns, such as the potential conflict in the South China Sea and the instability of the Korean Peninsula have heightened the requirement of institutionalising arrangements and preventive diplomacy designed to resolve potential crisis. The Korean Peninsula is, therefore, an active security concern for ASEAN in particular and the Asia Pacific in general. The breakdown of the Six-Party talks has resulted in one less avenue for engaging North Korea. More importantly, the talks failed to denuclearise North Korea which leads to discomfort for its neighbouring states in the region. Hence, the region has to ensure that any fallout from possible open conflict in the Korean Peninsula should be mitigated, if not contained.

Conclusion

To maintain high, sustainable economic growth in the Asia Pacific region, nations need to control their own strategies within an international context in the post-economic crisis period. It is essential to strengthen cooperation at the regional level and define new requests, forms and scope in accordance with the changing dynamics. The Asia Pacific region has the capacity to be a global driver especially since global power tilt towards Asia is unmistakable. While the US and Europe remain influential, Asia's unbridled capacity for growth has pushed it to the forefront. The changing regional security environment will have an impact on how Asia Pacific can lead the region. The trends of the last decade indicate that this new century will be dominated by the power of technology and a globalised economic system. It is inevitable that the global socio-economic centre of gravity should shift to Asia. The Asia Pacific region has to respond creatively to absorb this change through a web of cooperative arrangements that would promote this transition in a stable manner.

The challenges to the region are multifarious and multifaceted, that range from economic security issues to traditional and non-traditional ones. Most importantly, they cannot be easily resolved by pure economic and security powers alone. South East Asia in tandem with East Asia is likely to be the arena of future power tussles and confrontation between China and the US. There may not be armed conflict but a state of Cold War is likely to persist. At the same time, if China indulges in strategic and military brinkmanship, localised armed conflicts may occur. Major Powers must realise that a region, where only a single power or even a concert of powers can decide the affairs and the direction of cooperation, will not be acceptable. They also need to intensify their own cooperation efforts and stop a revival of a Cold War mentality that further destabilises the region. Incremental improvements in state relations can assure a stressed region that peace and stability are indeed shared goals. The challenge is to carefully consider the direction, the structure and the function of any future regional security architecture through renewed diplomatic and defence initiatives and increased contacts among leaders. An assessment of the confidence built around the ARF is necessary and will be a good first step.

Session II
Third Paper (Auditorium)

Sr Col Vu Van Khanh (Vietnam)

An Assessment of Political, Security and Economic Architecture in the Asia Pacific Region

The paper is divided into four parts, namely: Introduction, Political and Security Architecture, Economic Architecture and Conclusion

Introduction

Security architecture can be defined as an overall combination of organisations, mechanisms and arrangements, processes etc that maintain peace and stability. The two key ways to operationalise this is through bilateral arrangements and multilateral mechanisms. Moreover, security architecture can be realised in two main areas, that of political and security and secondly in the economic realm.

Political and Security Architecture

The political and security architecture of the Asia Pacific region, in the first half of the twentieth century was shaped by Cold War concerns. The strategic triangle of the US, Russia and China dictated the fortunes of the region. It was also a time of bilateral relations with the US, like that of US-Japan, US-South Korea, US-Philippines, US-Russia etc. After the Cold War, security cooperation has become the popular trend. The new regional architecture has had new developments and focusses on the harmony of many powers in the region. Currently, Sino-US relations are the most important factor shaping the security architecture in the region. The other big powers are US, Russia, Japan etc, but their foreign relations are still influenced by Sino-US dynamics.

On the other hand, the nature of Sino-US relation is between an emerging power and a declining power. China has potential to become a super power, but unlike in the Cold War period, these two powers are increasingly dependent on the other in terms of economy and realise the importance of working together on regional security issues. Although relations between them tend to develop cracks, these are unlikely to breakdown completely. Since both are keen to maintain peace, stability and prosperity, the security architecture in the Asia-Pacific region looks set to develop progressively.

Among the components in this new security architecture, bilateral relations continue to play the leading role. Currently there are bilateral arrangements between US-Japan, US-South Korea, US-Philippines, US-Australia etc. These coalitions have not yet combined into a network of multilateral defence like the NATO. This is the main difference between the security architecture in the Asia-Pacific region and the Atlantic.

In the West, the NATO and OSCE are the primary security and political mechanisms. In this region, the multilateral mechanisms operating are of two types. The first is based on the coordination role of ASEAN. They are tagged under ASEAN + 1, ASEAN + 3, EAS, ARF, ASEAN Defence Ministers Meetings + 1 etc. The second type is of the APEC, TPP, Shanghai Cooperation Organisation etc.

In the medium term, these mechanisms will continue to exist, complementing and competing, but it is unlikely that they will emerge to play the foremost role in the security of the region. The limited role of the multilateral mechanisms will continue to be the weakness of regional cooperation in the Asia-Pacific region, in the future.

The EAS has long been supported by Australia, India, Japan and other members; however, with the active participation of the US and Russia, the cooperation process in the EAS can be speeded up to move faster than the other arrangements currently existing. The advantage of the high level endorsement can allow the EAS to emerge as a key forum for dialogue and security cooperation in the region. It is complimented by the ADM and the AIF +. In political and security cooperation, EAS and AIF will focus on political issues, while ADM + will focus on specialised issues like HA/DR, maritime security, military exercises, counter-terrorism and peace keeping operations.

Regional Economic Architecture

Recently, there have been some noticeable features in the regional economic architecture. ASEAN continues to support the establishment of Free Trade Areas (FTAs) between ASEAN and outside countries, in which ASEAN plays a central role. However as a matter of fact, the ASEAN + 1 and FTA formula has not achieved the desired effect, as FTA has been established with lower levels of integration. The weaknesses of this kind of FTA will have negative impact on ASEAN's economic credibility in the region. In addition, the limited economic potential of ASEAN makes it difficult to promote multilateral economic cooperation in the region.

At present, the TPP and APEC remain as two mechanisms with the role to link the economic architecture of the two important coasts. With the recent impetus by the US, TPP is regarded as a new factor in multilateral economic cooperation in this region. In the near future, TPP will be less likely to replace APEC as it is not extended to all APEC members. However, if the TPP negotiations move smoothly with prospective countries like Japan and South Korea, then the TPP will possibly become the key liberalising mechanism in the Asia-Pacific region. On the other hand, the development of TPP runs the risk of the breakdown of ASEAN, as not all ASEAN members participate in the TPP negotiations.

For Vietnam, the effort has been to consistently implement its foreign policy guidelines of independence, peace and cooperation, development, multilateralisation, foreign policy openness and diversification of international relations, Vietnam has always advocated close cooperation among nations, especially with countries of the region, to settle all issues of national, regional and international security, based on equality and mutual benefit through multilateral mechanisms.

However, Vietnam does not support the formation of military alliances in the region as alliance raises suspicion which is not conducive to stability in the region. In future, in order to advance cooperation in the region in a favourable manner and for peace and security in each country, the regional cooperation mechanisms must be in compliance with the UN Charter and International law. The establishment of regional cooperation mechanism must conform to the conditions and capabilities of each country. All participants have to cooperate and respect benefits for community and individuals. It is important to respect sovereignty, territorial integrity, non interference in internal affairs, as well as appreciate cooperation and its benefits.

Session II (Seminar Room 1)
Chairman's Opening Remarks

Professor Richard Rigby (Australia)

We have about fifteen minutes for each speaker. And I should start by asking Mr. Hideki Asari, from Japan, to begin. He is currently Deputy Director General in the Institute of International Affairs, but he, like me, has had much of his career in diplomacy. I would skip his CV because it would take a long time to go through that. So, without much ado I would ask Mr. Asari to begin.

Session II

First Paper (Seminar Room 1)

Mr Hideki Asari (Japan)

Existing political and economic frameworks in the Asia-Pacific

The past two decades have seen a growth of regional frameworks in the Asia-Pacific region. Originally as a move on an economic front, the APEC (Asia-Pacific Economic Cooperation) was established in its first Ministerial meeting in Canberra, in 1989. It has been expanded to include all the major powers of the region minus India, including the US, Japan, China and Russia and now taking on an ambitious goal of creating a region-wide free trade area as well as working on a non-traditional security aspect of regional cooperation. After the relatively long period of modest development, the APEC gained its momentum by the enhanced US commitment to the Asia-Pacific region, as shown by Secretary Clinton's contribution to the Foreign Policy (November 2011). The APEC leaders agreed on the ambitious Yokohama Vision last year and the US hosting this year's Leaders meeting in Hawaii, which is continuing as of today, is symbolic of its commitment to this framework.

The development of a regional framework on a security front came into being a little later, when the first Ministerial meeting of the ARF (ASEAN Regional Forum) was held in 1994. Initiated as an ASEAN initiative in the wake of the end of the Cold War, the ARF is now the regional framework specialising in security affairs and covering all the major powers of the region. This framework is also unique in that it includes such countries as North Korea. At its second Ministerial meeting in 1995, the ARF members agreed on the "Three Step Approach" for its role to maintain peace and stability of the region, namely, (i) confidence building, (ii) preventive diplomacy and (iii) an approach to conflict and making steady (or slow, depending on the viewpoint) progress. The ARF has also been working on such issues as non-proliferation, counter-terrorism and disaster response. In March this year, the ARF Disaster Relief Exercise (DiRex) was conducted in Indonesia, with the participation of more than 4,000 personnel from 25 countries, regions and organisations.

The EAS (East Asia Summit) is a more recent product of regional cooperation. Inaugurated in 2005 in Kuala Lumpur, it will include all the major powers of the region by welcoming the leaders of the United States and Russia for the first time this year in the Bali meeting, on November 19. The priority areas for the EAS have been finance, education, energy, disaster management and avian flu prevention, but the EAS is expected to play a greater role in security areas such as maritime security and non-proliferation.

The Asia-Pacific region has seen other frameworks which are more limited in membership and scopes, but nonetheless important. The Six-Party Talk, created in 2003, is an important vehicle for achieving "the verifiable denuclearisation of the Korean Peninsula in a peaceful manner". There have also been frameworks of trilateral cooperation such as the US-Japan-Australia and the US-Japan-ROK which complement both bilateral cooperation and cooperation in the fora which is more multilateral. Of course one shall be amiss if proper credit is not given to ASEAN (Association of South-East Asian Nations), the framework in this region which is by far much older than others. Though sometimes criticised for slow consensus-based decision-making system described as "ASEAN Way", it has proved itself as an effective framework of regional cooperation both in terms of political/security and economic factors. In particular, a remarkable economic progress of the ASEAN countries can be partly attributed to various economic and trade initiatives, some of which involve non-ASEAN economic partners.

Further on an economic side, one can also see a web of free trade agreements both bilateral and multilateral. Sometimes criticised as aberration from the multilateral free trading system or "spaghetti bowl" that makes business transaction more complicated, these free trade agreements can be regarded as frameworks that have helped regional economic integration. TPP (Trans-Pacific Partnership) Agreement now negotiated by nine countries of the region, is one of the newest attempts in this context. Japan's participation in the TPP, as expressed by Prime Minister Noda last week, will give further weight to this framework.

How effective are these frameworks —Have they fulfilled regional aspiration?

To answer this question, one should first ascertain what "regional aspiration" is, or if that "aspiration" is relevant. Any regional framework building should be the right reflection of the regional reality, as building frameworks for the sake of building them is of no avail. One of the striking differences between Europe and Asia-Pacific is that the latter is yet to possess essential qualities of the "community", namely a similar level of economic development, shared values and maybe "post-modernness" of the societies. The last quality needs some clarification. Robert Cooper characterised the post-modern world as possessing such characteristic as breaking down of the distinction between domestic and foreign affairs and mutual interference of (traditional) domestic affairs and mutual surveillance, which one may say, is by and large, characteristic of the states comprising the European Union. On the other hand, the Asia-Pacific region can be described as the collection of states, some of which are nearing toward the post-modern phase while some others are in a typical stage of modern "Westphalia" nation-state. Furthermore, I may not be the only one to say that the value of democracy and human rights are yet to be fully shared in the Asia-Pacific.

The "regional aspiration" should be put correctly in the particular context of the Asia-Pacific as described above. The region of "modern" nation states with conflicting interests needs both a superpower or balancer which provide the most important public good, namely security, as well as frameworks of regional cooperation to expand and work on common interest. This is why the Asia-Pacific region needs the US commitment and effective functioning of the bilateral alliances between the US and its allies.

What, then, are the roles of political and economic frameworks in the Asia-Pacific, against which the effectiveness or performance of the existing frameworks is to be assessed? That the Asia-Pacific is yet to reach the stage of "community" as seen in Europe does not mean that this region cannot aspire to be a "community". On the contrary, an economic integration in the Asia-Pacific has progressed at a very remarkable speed, turning this region as the economic power-house of the world and raising the living standards of the people and gradually creating a sense of "community" among the members of this region. This remarkable economic integration is partly a result of industrial policies in the region and corporate behaviour, for instance, an increase of Japanese direct investment in the wake of appreciation of yen in the late 1980's, but the continuous effort of economic integration by ASEAN members and free trade agreements as well as joint endeavour towards economic integration under the APEC, should also deserve credit.

On the other hand, achievement may be somewhat modest on the security front. The ARF, having been in place for more than fifteen years, is still in the very initial phase of the second stage, preventive diplomacy. The activities of the EAS on the security front are, till date, limited to the issue of non-traditional security such as disaster management and avian flu, though there is increasing support for the EAS, playing more role in maritime security and non-proliferation. Having said that, the regional fora do provide important venues for confidence building. By working closely on non-traditional security issues such as disaster response, the countries of the region have succeeded in expanding their common interest and become more used to working together, to this end. Even on more controversial issues such as the dispute in the South China Sea, the relevant parties have successfully established the guideline to implement the Declaration of Conduct of Parties in the South China Sea and now working on the Code of Conduct, the move partly facilitated by the discussion in the ARF Ministerial meeting in 2010. Also, the very fact that leaders and ministers meet regularly and officials working closely on regional security issues are conducive to creating a collegiate sense of cooperation.

In sum, the achievement of various frameworks in the Asia-Pacific is varied, especially if one compares the achievement on the security front and economic front. However, one may at least say that these frameworks, be it security or economics, provide an important infrastructure of the regional security, namely, economic prosperity, maintaining confidence and gradual growth of sense of "community".

Session II
Second Paper (Seminar Room 1)
Professor Moon Jangnyeol (South Korea)

Northeast Asia is a small part of the Asia-Pacific geography but its political and economic gravity is large. This region includes five resident states, namely, South and North Koreas, China, Japan and Russia, all the world's major military and/or economic powers. In addition, the US, from outside, plays a crucial role in the regional security and economic matters.

Into the 21st century, Northeast Asia has not seen any official regional cooperation framework in which all six states participate. Some say it is because of the legacy of the past history yet to be cleared up and others point out strategic competitions between big powers. Considering the growing economy, maturing democracy, internal social changes and globalisation, this region needs such a multilateral framework now more than ever. Perhaps the Northeast Asia Cooperation Dialogue (NEACD) which started in 1993 is the only forum that all the six states are meant to participate in. But it still remains semi-official, or track 1.5 with North Korea's seat empty.

Recently, however, all the above-mentioned six states have been endeavouring to solve the North Korean nuclear problem through the so-called Six-Party Talks. As of now it is far from being successful in denuclearising North Korea after seven and a half years since the first round of the Talks. Nevertheless, in the course of the Talks, this framework showed a possibility that it could evolve into a more substantive regional mechanism for political and economic cooperation. We review, in this paper, significant agreements reached in the Six-Party Talks, supporting such a possibility and assess it in a few important aspects.

An overview of the Six-Party Talks:

US-DPRK negotiations and the 1994 Agreed Framework

The so-called first North Korean nuclear crisis began when their nuclear activities were known to the world in 1989 via the French commercial satellite SPOT. International pressure, IAEA inspections and North Korea's protest ensued subsequently. Finally, the US-DPRK bilateral negotiations reached an agreement in 1994 known as the Geneva Agreed Framework, the main points of which are as follows:

- North Korea freezes nuclear facilities and reaccepts IAEA inspections.
- KEDO (Korea Energy Development Organisation) is to be formed to provide North Korea with two lightwater reactors, with a capacity of one million kilowatts each.
- The US provides North Korea with 500,000 tons of heavy oil each year until the reactors are in operation.
- Both North Korea and the US endeavour to normalise their relations.

Second nuclear crisis and the formation of the Six-Party Talks

The progress of implementing the Agreed Framework was rather slow except for the US annual support of heavy oil for North Korea. In the mean time, North Korea test-fired a long-range ballistic missile known as Daepodong in August 1998. Although some quick and focussed efforts were made to spur up the Agreed Framework between the US and North Korea in the latter part of Clinton Administration, all the positive developments suddenly halted as of 2001. President Bush declared to include North Korea in the "axis of evil" and North Korea vehemently protested against it.

The real demise of the faltering Agreed Framework was then presumed when the US State Department Deputy Assistant Secretary, James Kelly, visited North Korea and accused it of having been carrying out a clandestine highly enriched uranium (HEU) program, which according to his report North Korea "acknowledged." The US immediately suspended the heavy oil supply and North Korea, in return, lifted the nuclear freeze, expelled IAEA inspectors and then withdrew from the NPT in January 2003, which is often dubbed as the second North Korean nuclear crisis. This time China volunteered and endeavoured to play a role of showing its good offices in addressing this crisis. After a tripartite meeting among North Korea, the US and China held in April 2003, the Six-Party Talks officially came into being.

Major events and agreements during the Six-Party Talks

The whole course of the Six-Party Talks is very complex, now being in a long stalemate. So we will just recount some major events and agreements which are significant for more meaningful assessments and further discussions. The first three rounds of the Talks, convened in 2003 and 2004, were essentially an open arena of disputes between North Korea and the US. The US demanded the complete, verifiable and irreversible dismantlement (CVID) of North Korea's nuclear program, while North Korea requested US official security assurance by, for instance, a non-aggression treaty.

Year 2005 saw a founding agreement reached on 19 September, called 9·19 Joint Statement, through painful efforts of South Korea after several months' deadlock of the Talks since North Korea declared in February that it possessed nuclear weapons and would keep increasing its arsenal. The 9·19 Joint Statement included, among other things:

- All state parties are in consensus on the verifiable and peaceful denuclearisation of North Korea.
- The US and Japan will normalise their relations with North Korea.
- The state parties will launch energy and economic cooperation for North Korea with two million kilowatts of electric power.
- The state parties will commit themselves to regional peace and stability including the establishment of the "Korean Peninsula Peace Regime."
- The implementation of the agreement shall be carried out step-by-step and in mutually coordinated actions.

This mechanism could not be practiced in due course because, this time, the US Department of Treasury froze the North Korean account at Banco Delta, Asia in Macau, claiming it to be related to illicit activities, upon which North Korea demanded the US to lift economic sanctions. Without getting any positive answer from the US, North Korea demonstrated its protest by carrying out a nuclear test in October 2006. Scrambled and busy again, the Six-Party Talks produced another agreement in four months' time, on 13 February 2007. This 2·13 Agreement reconfirmed the 9·19 Joint Statement and specified its concrete implementation actions, including North Korea's freeze, declaration and disablement of nuclear programs and facilities. It also formed five working groups for better implementation of the 9·19 Joint Statement, whose titles are: denuclearisation of the Korean Peninsula, normalisation of North Korea-US relations, normalisation of North Korea-Japan relations, economic and energy cooperation and a peace and security regime for Northeast Asia.

There was very little progress in implementing the above agreements until the US Government removed North Korea from the State Sponsors of Terrorism List in October 2008 and North Korea agreed on basic principles of verification for its denuclearisation. However, the details of verification measures could not be agreed upon during the Six-Party Talks delegations meeting held in December 2008, after which no more Six-Party Talks have been convened until now.

In the mean time, South Korea saw a new administration launched in February 2008 led by President Lee Myung-bak, who abandoned the Sunshine Policy as a fruitless appeasement and took a tough stance toward North Korea. The inter-Korean relation rapidly deteriorated. The new Obama Administration did not actively engage in the negotiations with North Korea which is contrary to the widely held anticipation. It seems that Washington is determined to go in concert with its ally, South Korea, insofar as the North Korea policy is concerned, while continuing to focus on the war on terror in the Middle East and internal problems.

In April 2009, North Korea openly launched a space rocket, dubbed "Eunha II," which was known to have failed in placing a satellite in orbit.

Two weeks later, all the IAEA inspectors monitoring the nuclear activities withdrew from North Korea. Another month later, on 25 May 2009, North Korea carried out its second nuclear test. Into the year 2010, North Korea seemed to take a double-track approach to the Six-Party Talks. On the one hand, it officially proposed in January to conclude a peace treaty replacing the Armistice Agreement for the official termination of the Korean War among relevant state parties. Kim Jong Il expressed his hope for the Six-Party Talks to reopen as early as possible, when he visited China in May and August. On the other hand, in November, North Korea invited Charles L. Pritchard, a former special envoy for negotiations with North Korea and Siegfried S. Hecker, a Stanford professor and nuclear scientist and showed them their new uranium enrichment facility with two thousand centrifuges.

Recent developments for resuming the Six-Party Talks

In 2011, there have been some developments toward the resumption of the Six-Party Talks. Barak Obama and Hu Jintao agreed on the necessity of resuming the Six-Party Talks in the Washing summit held in January. In April, North Korean and Chinese head representatives met in Beijing and reached an agreement on the three-stage process to resume the Six-Party Talks, which South Korea and the US consented to. The three stages are first inter-Korean dialogue, second North Korea-US dialogue and then third, the Six-Party Talks. Kim Jong Il repeatedly stressed on reopening of the Talks as early as possible and without any preconditions, as in the former US president Jimmy Carter's visit to North Korea in April, North Korea-China summit in May and North Korea-Russia summit in August.

Currently, the inter-Korean dialogues under the title of "South and North Korean Denuclearisation Talk" and the North Korea-US contacts are being held in parallel. The two Koreas had the first meeting in Bali, Indonesia, in July and second in Beijing, in September. North Korean and US high officials had contacts in New York in July and in Geneva, in October. In such dialogues, South Korea and the US demand North Korea to suspend the uranium enrichment program, to reaccept the IAEA inspectors and to declare a moratorium of WMD tests as a precondition. But North Korea apparently rejects any preconditions for resuming the Six-Party Talks.

An assessment of the Six-Party Talks Framework

If we attempt to assess the Six-Party Talks Framework at the present, we immediately see 'the mission unaccomplished.' The main objective of the Talks, namely denuclearisation of North Korea, has failed. North Korea tested the nuclear explosion twice, possibly manufactured a few nuclear bombs, tested long-range ballistic missiles in the guise of satellite launch rockets and built a modern uranium enrichment facility.

Other important objectives stipulated in the 9·19 Joint Statement also remain incomplete or, admittedly, worsened. Bilateral relations of North Korea with the US and Japan made little progress towards normalisation. Economic and energy cooperation among the states and North Korea has stopped while the UN sanctions against North Korea have been strengthened. This seems to have entailed such a deep political and economic dependency of North Korea on China that the Chinese Government might feel burdened. Discussions on establishing the Korean Peninsula Peace Regime and a regional peace and security regime did not even start.

An analysis of the failure

There are many factors that have prevented the Six-Party Talks from becoming a success. It could be the nature of North Korea and Kim Jong Il, or the South Korea's lack of competence, or the big powers' reluctance to active engagement, based on different strategic calculations. But it is hard to deny that the single most fundamental obstacle is the deep-rooted distrust, among the state parties, especially between North Korea and the US, the two key actors in the negotiation process. The lack of confidence naturally makes them reluctant to compromise on their strategic mismatch, to save each other's face and to move first. Standing on the brink of life and death with their own threat perception, North Korea may not be able to have much room for choosing any flexible negotiation tactics other than their 'good old,' or 'bad old,' brinkmanship. It has been repeated by North Korea every time the Six-Party Talks got bogged down and it is hard to deny that it worked.

Evolutionary potential for regional political and economic framework

Despite the failure of achieving the intended goals, the Six-Party Talks gained a potential to evolve into a regional political and economic cooperation framework as a set of goals, much broader than the nuclear issue, were defined in the 9·19 Joint Statement in 2005. It dictates the implementation of the agreement to be carried out 'step-by-step' and 'in mutually coordinated actions.' This principle should be applied not only to actions for denuclearisation but also to all the other political and economic actions.

The normalisation of North Korea's bilateral relations with the US and Japan will drastically lessen the military tension between the two sets of states. When the Korean Peninsula Peace Regime is established through negotiations among relevant state parties, the military confrontation between the two Koreas will practically disappear. These changes must have a great synergetic effect on one another and provide a scaffold for regional peace and security cooperation regime.

The economic and energy cooperation among the six state parties has even richer potential for the benefit of each state and the common prosperity of the region. North Korea has already designated a couple of special economy areas near the borders to China and Russia, to invite their investments. The connection of the Trans China Railroad and the Trans Siberia Railroad to Trans Korea Railroads is a long sought-after project, waiting for negotiations between the two Koreas. Connecting gas pipelines from Russia through North Korea to South Korea and Japan is another mega project. Incidentally, Kim Jong Il agreed on cooperating with Russia in this matter when he visited Russia in August 2010. All these economic and energy cooperations are demanding and must be expedited by the success of the Six-Party Talks Framework and its evolution into a regional cooperation regime.

Conclusion

Over more than 20 years, the North Korean nuclear problem has been dealt with, first in the North Korea-US bilateral framework and then in the multilateral Six-Party Talks. Presently, we must admit that no substantial achievement towards the goal have been made and the road ahead still looks long, winding and rocky. But those past years should not be regarded as a meaningless waste of time. Each state party had a good deal of chances to better understand each other. More importantly, we found a good potential of the Six-Party Talks to evolve into a regional political and economic cooperation framework in Northeast Asia. To turn such hope and aspiration into a reality, much more confidence building and active engagement among all the state parties will be essential.

Session II

Third paper (Seminar Room 1)

Dr Claudia Astarita (Italy)

Rare Earths: the New "Great Game"

Including rare earths trade in the discussion on peace and stability in Asia-Pacific Region can sound a bit surprising. However, it is a matter of fact that the exchange of strategic resources such as oil, gas and rare earths can significantly affect great powers' ideas on security architecture. Commercial security is just another aspect of non-traditional security and China right now is the only country that can afford mining enough rare earths to satisfy their growing global demand. As this chapter is going to show, during the last few years many countries eventually realised that China's near monopoly in minerals production can become dangerous. As a consequence, all nations that are currently highly dependent on imports from the People's Republic of China are looking for alternatives. This chapter shows that in medium-term, countries such as Australia, Malaysia, Canada and India can partially cover the global demand, but in the long-term only Russia and the United States have enough resources to counterbalance China, even though it is still not clear whether they are really interested in and capable of establishing themselves in this market.

China's Rise in Rare Earths Market

Rare earths are moderately abundant in the earth's crust, some of them even more abundant than copper, lead, gold and platinum. However, they are not concentrated enough to be easily exploitable economically. Except for yttrium and scandium, fifteen out of seventeen elements belong to the chemical group called lanthanides. The lanthanides consist of lanthanum, cerium, praseodymium, neodymium, promethium, samarium, europium, gadolinium, terbium, dysprosium, holmium, erbium, thulium, ytterbium and lutetium. Some of the major end uses for rare earth elements include automotive catalytic converters, fluid cracking catalysts in petroleum refining, phosphors in colour television and flat panel displays, permanent magnets and rechargeable batteries for hybrid and electric vehicles, generators for wind turbines and numerous medical devices. Further, there are important defence applications, such as jet fighter engines, missile guidance systems, antimissile defence, space-based satellites and communication systems that cannot function without rare earths.

Large-scale mining of rare earths began in the 1950s, with most of the world's production coming from a mine at Mountain Pass, in California, a desert region near the Nevada border. Much of the early demand came from the oil refining and glass manufacturing industries. Several years later, as soon as their magnetic properties were discovered, new applications were found and rare earths started being extensively used by hi-tech industries. When this happened, China decided to step into the market and after a few years, it started selling rare earths at cheaper prices than any other producer, pushing them out of the market.

Rare Earth Elements (Lanthanides): Selected End Use			
Light Rare Earths (more abundant)	**Major End Use**	**Heavy Rare Earth (less abundant)**	**Major End Use**
Lanthanum	hybrid engines, metal alloys	Terbium	phosphors, permanent magnets
Cerium	auto catalyst, petroleum refining, metal alloys	Dysprosium	permanent magnets, hybrid engines
Praseodymium	magnets	Erbium	phosphors
Neodymium	auto catalyst, petroleum refining, hard drives inl aptops, headphones, hybrid engines	Yttrium	red colour, fluorescent lamps, ceramics, metal alloy agent
Samarium	magnets	Holmium	glass colouring, lasers
Europium	red colour for television and computer screens	Thulium	medical x-ray units
		Lutetium	catalysts in petroleum refining
		Ytterbium	lasers, steel alloys
		Gadolinium	magnets

Source: DOI, U.S. Geological Survey, Circular 930-N.

In 2008, the European Commission published a document, "The Raw Materials Initiative - Meeting our Critical Needs for Growth and Jobs in Europe", listing some materials, including rare earths, which in a few years are likely to become rare. Brussels argues that if China, India and Brazil will keep their actual growth rates, their international demand will rise by at least twenty times.

Rare earths have recently become a source of concern for Western countries for two reasons. First, the mining process is expensive because of rare earths low concentration in minerals and to complete it, it is necessary to use dangerous acids that can produce large quantities of toxic waste. Second is the awareness that in the '90s, the People's Republic of China replaced the United States as the main global rare earths supplier, increasing its market quota from 27 to 97 per cent by 2009. Further, Western countries are worried because since China detains 55 per cent of rare earths reserves, it might start exploiting this strategic advantage to bargain some political and economic grants. After all, thirty years ago, the then Party Secretary Deng Xiaoping, the father of Chinese economic reforms, worried the West reminding it of the fact that the "Middle East has oil, but China has rare earths".

Today, the world is aware of how dangerous leaving any country with a near-monopoly on rare earths can be. Accordingly, both Europe and the United States are trying to find alternative solutions to reduce Chinese extensive power in this market. It is worth remembering at this stage that although Japan has been the main rare earths importer since 1999, among the fifteen biggest importers there are eight Western countries. Italy is now the tenth importer in the world, after its 12 million Euro imports in 2010, after the United States (146.8), Germany (71.9), France (51), Canada (28.8) and the Netherlands (16.2) and followed by the United Kingdom (12) and Spain (9.5).

	Rare earths imports (million Euros)											
	1999	2000	2001	2002	2003	2004	2005	2006	2007	2008	2009	2010
Japan	149.7	241.9	168.7	136.8	123.5	153.1	176.6	292.6	430.5	384.7	164.5	585.1
United States	133.7	152.9	153.9	98.3	82.0	77.4	79.7	83.6	98.3	132.6	82.5	146.7
Germany	35.4	48.2	43.1	28.0	27.4	25.4	27.0	30.6	36.8	51.2	39.3	71.9
France	28.2	31.4	72.2	24.7	23.8	24.8	21.5	73.0	50.7	45.3	32.4	51.0
South Korea	22.6	33.9	36.4	37.3	29.1	27.1	23.5	19.5	17.2	17.5	18.1	44.4
China	18.4	26.3	18.3	12.4	15.8	23.9	27.0	37.8	59.3	19.0	24.9	28.0
Canada	4.1	7.5	6.8	8.4	8.6	7.3	5.6	3.2	3.1	4.0	3.0	28.8
The Netherlands	6.0	13.2	22.1	12.3	13.8	12.2	16.5	21.3	35.7	24.7	9.6	16.2
Taiwan	11.6	16.9	19.6	20.2	22.5	18.0	16.1	14.1	11.7	11.5	11.5	13.5
Italy	8.9	10.0	8.3	6.6	6.3	6.1	10.6	7.8	11.3	10.9	7.5	12.0
Malaysia	6.1	9.3	7.2	6.9	4.1	5.1	2.4	2.9	2.3	6.5	8.0	9.6
United Kingdom	18.7	19.7	20.4	21.6	15.5	13.3	14.4	9.0	15.0	13.2	7.2	12.0
Spain	3.9	4.0	5.0	4.2	3.7	4.2	5.1	6.2	8.3	7.9	3.4	9.5
Singapore	12.2	28.0	22.9	25.6	14.0	1.4	1.6	9.4	5.3	3.4	5.9	8.2
Hong Kong	9.6	4.3	6.5	4.0	5.4	6.7	4.6	8.1	24.2	15.3	3.6	10.6
World	469.1	647.5	611.4	447.6	395.5	406.0	432.2	619.1	809.7	747.7	421.4	1047.5

Source: WTA-GTI-ICE

The Problem of Rare Earths Supply Vulnerability

World demand for rare earth elements is estimated at 136,000 tons per year, with global production of around 133,600 tons in 2010. Until now, the difference has been covered by previously mined aboveground stocks. However, since world demand is projected to rise to at least 185,000 tons annually by 2015, rare earths prices will probably keep on increasing. Even though experts expect that global reserves and undiscovered resources are large enough to meet demand, it is evident that every country that will manage to increase its internal production will benefit from rare earths trade.

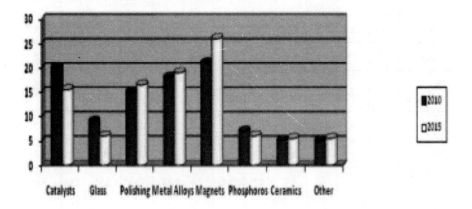

Figure 1: Rare Earths Demand by Application. World 2010 and 2015
Source: IMCOA, 2011

Rare earths production concentration raises the important issue of supply vulnerability. Today's production is concentrated in China (95%). The Chinese government has said with increasing frequency that it wants to limit rare earths exports to protect the environment, preserve its own reserves, fight illegal mining and sales and encourage the development of manufacturing within China. The Ministry of Industry and Information Technology even circulated a draft plan in 2009 to ban the export of five rare earths, but the Chinese government later retreated from this idea under international pressure. In early November, Beijing decided to suspend the operations in its main mine, Baotau (47 % of total production), in Inner Mongolia, aiming at stabilising market prices after their collapse during the summer of 2011. From July on, cerium had lost 48 per cent of its value, lanthanum, 36 per cent and neodymium, 22 per cent. One-month suspension at the Baotou plant implies, removing from the global market, 5.000 tons of rare earths. This choice could create such an impact on the international market to raise prices faster.

Rare Earths prices (US$ per kilo)						
Rare earth	Purity	1995	2000	2005	2008	2009
Cerium	96.00	3,8	19,2	19,2	50,0	30,0
Dysprosium	96.00	27,0	120,0	120,0	160,0	170,0
Erbium	98.00	29,3	155,0	155,0	165,0	100,0
Europium	99.99	202,5	990,0	990,0	1.200,0	1.600,0
Gadolinium	99.99	24,8	130,0	130,0	150,0	150,0
Holmium	99.90	-	440,0	440,0	750,0	750,0
Lanthanum	99.99	3,9	23,0	23,0	40,0	30,0
Lutetium	99.99	-	3.500,0	3.500,0	3.500,0	1.800,0
Neodymium	95.00	4,7	28,5	28,5	60,0	42,0
Praseodymium	96.00	7,6	36,8	36,8	75,0	38,0
Samarium	96.00	13,5	360,0	360,0	200,0	130,0
Terbium	99.90	168,8	535,0	535,0	850,0	900,0
Thulium	90.90	-	2.500,0	2.300,0	2.500,0	1.500,0
Ytterbium	99.00	-	230,0	340,0	450,0	325,0
Yttrium	99.99	22,5	88,0	88,0	50,0	44,0

Source: USGS

It should be noted that rare earths prices have always been very high. The values of certain minerals increased ten times in just three years. There are two reasons behind the recent collapse of rare earths demand: the earthquake in Japan and the international financial crisis. The former has suddenly reduced imports from the world's largest consumer of rare earths. The latter further complicated the scenario since many countries specialised in hi-tech productions are recovering extremely slowly. It is not a coincidence that rare earths demand had dropped from 125 thousand tons in 2010 to 120 thousand in 2011. Outside China, the estimated consumption of sixty thousand tons has been reduced to forty. However, since price reduction affected not only the export market but also the Chinese, it is reasonable to argue that rare earths prices have been manipulated by internal speculators who decided to accumulate more stocks than usual, as a precautionary measure and afterwards had to sell everything altogether, fearing that a governmental inspection would confirm their previous reluctance to put on the market, the total amount of rare earths produced.

China's Rare Earth Production and Exports, 2006-2011						
	2006	2007	2008	2009	2010	2011
Official Chinese production quota	86,520	87,020	87,620	82,320	89,200	93,800
USGS reported production	119,000	120,000	120,000	129,000	130,000	112,500 (estimation)
Chinese export quota	61,560	60,173	47,449	50,145	30,259	30,246

Source: China Ministry of Land and Resources. U.S. Geological Survey. Ministry of Commerce of China.

Note: USGS production data exceeded Chinese quotas, some of which is attributed to illegal mining.

Reminding all of how much Beijing has reduced its rare earths export quotas in the last ten years, Brussels has recently tried to convince the international community to punish China for its anti-commercial policy. Several times, although with limited results, Brussels tried to involve the World Trade Organisation in the rare earths exports issue. Further, in January, the European Commission warned that the EU could unilaterally suspend the generalised system of preferences to any country applying unjustified restriction to strategic materials exports.

Something changed in July 2011, when the WTO eventually affirmed that China's export restrictions on a series of key industrial minerals, including rare earths, are not justified on environmental grounds and should be lifted. Ending a case initiated by the EU and the US in June 2009, the WTO report shows that China has not respected commitments made upon its accession to the organisation in 2001, when it agreed to eliminate all export duties, except for a number of products listed separately and promised not to apply new export quotas.

Although China has claimed that in this case export restrictions are necessary to preserve exhaustible natural resources and reduce harmful emissions of carbon dioxide, the WTO is now insisting on China to conform to its international obligation. Indeed, while the EU and the US complain that export quotas are discouraging the export of rare earths, reducing supply lines and making their prices too high, the same is not happening in China, where they are cheap and easily available to the domestic market. Similarly, the WTO noted that export restrictions cannot be based on environmental concerns, essentially because the production and the domestic consumption of these materials in China are not restricted.

The day after the WTO clarified that China cannot shield domestic producers from foreign competition in the name of conservation, the Chinese Ministry of Commerce announced that it was ready to take "proper follow-up action in line with WTO practices".

To avoid depending on the Chinese near-monopoly, Brussels recently started focussing on a new strategy aimed at investing in new mines (even though China holds 97 per cent of today's rare earths production, in terms of deposits it has only 55 per cent) in the United State as well as in Vietnam,

Sweden, Africa and Greenland, whose mines might be able to provide, annually, one third of today's production. The United States holds about 13 per cent of world reserves, according to the most recent estimate. South Africa and Canada have significant rare earths potential and reserves are also found in Australia, Brazil, India, Russia, Malaysia, Mongolia and Malawi. Finally, Europe wants to invest in research to make the mining process easier and less expensive and to strengthen its rare earths recycling ability, leaving to Japan and the United States the charge of testing new material which might replace these minerals.

Rare Earth Elements: World Production and Reserves—2010						
Country	Mine Production (metric tons)	% of total	Reserves- (million metric tons)	% of total	Reserve Base (million metric tons)	% of total
United States	none		13.0	13	14.0	9.3
China	130,000	97.3	55.0	50	89.0	59.3
Russia (and other former Soviet Union countries)			19.0	17	21.0	14
Australia			1.6	1.5	5.8	3.9
India	2,700	2	3.1	2.8	1.3	1
Brazil	550	0.42	Small			
Malaysia	350	0.27	Small			
Other	NA		22.0	20	23	12.5
Total	133,600		110.0		154	

Source: U.S. Department of the Interior, Mineral Commodity Summaries, USGS, 2010.

Reserve Base is defined by the USGS to include reserves (both economic and marginally economic) plus some subeconomic resources (i.e., those that may have potential for becoming economic reserves).

New Actors in Rare Earths Market

Despite all European and American statements confirming their intention to scratch China's near-monopoly in rare earths production and trade, the only country that has come up as a real alternative to China is Malaysia. At the beginning of 2011, 2,500 workers were recruited to complete the world's largest rare earths refinery, the only one built outside China's boundaries during the last thirty years. Kuala Lumpur has decided to work on a plant that might change the future of the nation, aware that many countries would be willing to buy rare earths in Malaysia in order to reduce their dependence on China.

The reason why at the moment Malaysia remains the only country interested in joining rare earths mining industry is linked to the consciousness that the extraction process usually produces thousands of tons of radioactive waste. Aware of these risks, most countries have always preferred to let China deal with the "dirty work". The mining of rare earths has been largely unregulated and cause considerable environmental damage. Only in 2010, did the Chinese government start to take a series of steps to try and limit production, close illegal mines and consolidate the industry under the control of state-owned enterprises.

Today many things have changed and no country can afford leaving China with its near-monopoly in rare earths production. The Malaysian project has been entirely funded with capitals coming from abroad. Financing Malaysian refinery, the Australian giant Lynas has been generously rewarded with twelve years of tax relief coming in exchange of the commitment to equip the Malaysian plant with advanced technologies able to handle radioactive waste. This was a predictable request, considering that the rare earths refinery previously build by the Japanese group Mitsubishi became, only in seven years, the most radioactive location in Asia and was suddenly closed in 1992 for security reasons. However, even though the new "environmentally safe" refinery was supposed to be ready for production in

August 2011, it fell behind schedule due to public opposition and regulatory reviews of the disposal plans for thousands of tons of low-level radioactive waste that the plant would produce annually.

Following the Malaysian example, India has recently become more active in the rare earths market. New Delhi signed its first cooperation agreement in this area with Japan, the country that more than any other has expressed a sense of urgency to secure new non-Chinese supplies, as until now Tokyo has received 82 per cent of its rare earths from the People's Republic of China. In October 2010, the Indo-Japan Comprehensive Economic Cooperation Agreement (CEPA) was signed, aimed at cutting tariffs on 94 per cent of bilateral trade within ten years and at making it easier for Japanese companies to invest in the development of rare earths plants in India. Six weeks after India's Prime Minister Manmohan Singh and Japanese Prime Minister Naoto Kan met in Tokyo, Japanese trading house Toyota Tsusho Corp., partly owned by Toyota Motor Corp., announced plans to construct a rare-earths processing plant in India, in the Vishakapatnam Industrial Development Zone, in the South Indian state of Andhra Pradesh, in cooperation with Indian Rare Earths Ltd.. State-owned Indian Rare Earths has not mined rare earths since 2004, but the company has recently set up another processing plant in Orissa with capacity to produce 11,000 tons by early next year.

In addition to the above mentioned project and other production plans of Indian Rare Earths, several other Indian companies, from the public and private sectors, with tacit support from the Government and with favourable market conditions, have already made plans to increase their own endeavours in this area. These companies are Kerala Minerals and Metals Ltd., Travancore Titanium Products Ltd., Cochin Minerals and Rutile Ltd., Beach Minerals Co. Pvt. Ltd. and V.B. Minerals and Resins Pvt. Ltd.

Even though India is the second largest exporter of rare earths in the world with a production of 2,700 metric tons of minerals, in terms of reserves it has only 2.8 per cent of the global amount of precious minerals. India, together with Malaysia or Australia, the countries that are currently producing rare earths, cannot expect to counterbalance China any time soon. In order to secure new supply lines that might effectively shake Beijing's monopoly, Unites States and Russia, together with other former Soviet Union countries, should enter the game of rare earth production and trade. These two countries have 13 and 19 per cent of rare earths mines respectively.

In a very significant development, earlier this year, the Varun Mines and Minerals Ltd. of the Varun Group of Mumbai has acquired 1011 mining blocks covering 6950 sq. kms. in Madagascar. From the first ten mining blocks, Varun Mines and Minerals have already found some 266.8 million tons of heavy minerals, comprising of Zirconium, Titanium, Thorium and Rare Earths. This could then be a major game changer in the global rare earths business.

As far as Russia is concerned, more and more analysts argue that China's decision to reduce exports of rare earth metals is an opportunity that Moscow cannot miss. The country is currently producing rare earth metals only as by-products. In northern Russia, for instance, the Lovozersk integrated mining-and-processing plant mines loparite ores, which contain a wide range of rare earths. Despite having the second largest explored reserves of rare earths in the world as well as the world's largest anticipated reserves, as possible reserves may exceed all the rest of the world's reserves combined, the special minerals business is merely auxiliary at the moment. This is happening because rare earths production facilities in Russia are concentrated in the hands of a few entrepreneurs who are apparently not interested in developing this sector, as until recently prices have been low and demand from makers of products such as smartphones and wind power stations are yet to boom. Today many things have changed and Russia is well placed to leverage its mining capabilities and associated infrastructures. However, it will take at least a decade to develop rare earth deposits and step into the breach that has been created since China chopped supply of the metals to the rest of the world, but many countries are ready to tap Russia's resources.

Regarding the United States, Washington is sure that rare earth shortage could pose a real threat to its hi-tech industries. There are actually two ways to avoid this potential outcome: reopen the long-idle mines and push other countries such as Australia, Canada, South Africa, Vietnam, Kazakhstan and Mongolia to boost their national productions.

According to latest reports, some major new sites are already under development in Australia and Canada. The most significant of these are the Mt. Weld and the Nolans projects in Australia and even bigger is the Hoidas Lake project in Sasketchwan, Northern Canada. Current estimates are that the Hoidas Lake project alone could produce over 10 per cent of North America's entire requirement of rare earths.

However, the real 'game changer' could well come from Afghanistan. A first order survey conducted in 2010 and 2011 by the US Geological Survey in the Khan Neshin area of troubled Helmand province revealed a conservative one million tons of lanthanum, cerium and neodymium in just one square kilometre. The estimated $7.4 billion worth of rare earths in Khan Neshin area is enough for many years of requirements of countries other than China. Of course more detailed studies and analyses would need to be done once peace is restored, but just the initial data clearly points to why India and all other countries need to remain heavily invested in a free and stable Afghanistan.

Going back to United States rare earths national production, it has already been mentioned that through the 1960s until the 1980s, the Mountain Pass rare earth mine in California was the leading world rare earths producer and some experts assume that, once reopened, this mine could provide more than enough rare earths to meet the US demand. The country has not produced any rare earths since 2002, when the Mountain Pass mine shut its doors due to an economically unfriendly market, the result of both environmental issues in California and competition with China, whose burgeoning production of rare earths drove prices for the minerals down.

Today's barriers to US rare earth industry redevelopment are linked to funds and research. The federal government recently started encouraging lenders currently upset by the global economic downturn to provide the necessary funds for the mine to reopen and to create new research centres focussing on rare earths exploration, processing and manufacturing. When China entered the rare earth market in the 1990s, industries in the United

States and elsewhere shut down as they could not face Chinese competition. The dismissal of their technical experts created today's "intellectual vacuum".

In 2008, Molycorp Minerals, based in Colorado, bought both the mine and associated production facilities in California. Molycorp has now announced that it will restart full operation at the Mountain Pass Mine, which means that 900 new jobs would be created and the company will produce 19,000 tons of rare earth oxides per year by the end of 2012, enough to supply a third of the gap between China's production and global demand. Further, thanks to the superior and environmentally friendly technologies that the company is developing, Molycorp should be able to compete with China.

Conclusion

Despite being aware that rare earths are critical for hi-tech industries as well as for national security, as they are essential for building many powerful weapons including the highly potent, electromagnetic ones now under development, US Energy Department has predicted that it may take as many as 15 years to break American dependence on Chinese supplies, calls for the nation to increase research and expand diplomatic contacts to find alternative sources and to develop ways to recycle the minerals or replace them with other materials. The same could be said either for Russia, referring to its interest to start mining rare earths, or to Europe, considering its idea to explore new mines as well as to focus on minerals recycling: they all need to wait for a long time to be able to counterbalance China in the rare earth market. Accordingly, at least for now they need to find a way to interact with the People's Republic of China in a more constructive way, remembering that even though no country can afford a rare earths shortage, Beijing cannot afford to stop exporting these minerals, too.

It is possible that by reducing rare earths exports, China is currently trying to avoid selling these strategic materials at a lower price and save the exports for a better time. At the same time, considering Chinese long-term interest in upgrading its national industrial production as well as the more recent call for foreign hi-tech industries to move their plants to China where rare earths could be available at a better price, it is reasonable to argue that the country will be soon in a better position to attract foreign know how, technologies and expertise, to subsequently exploit these tools to strengthen its industrial capacity and therefore, start selling to the world, valuable finished goods rather than lowly raw materials.

It seems that the United States, Europe and Russia need to choose now whether they want to invest on rare earths mining or not. It is a matter of fact that China's growth will progressively need more rare earths for its own industries, consequently reducing the country's availability for exports. Similarly, it is impossible to expect that while remaining the only significant rare earths supplier Beijing will stop benefiting from its current advantage. Accordingly, these materials being so crucial for economic development and national security, it is highly recommended that both Russia and the Unites States start investing again in rare earths "clean mining" and that Europe keeps on focussing on minerals recycling. In the meanwhile it will be possible to rely on alternative imports coming from India, Malaysia or Australia, a temporary solution due to these countries' limited amount of rare earths deposits. Only if the United States and Russia prove successful in rare earths "clean mining" will they be able to meet their own industrial needs and offer the world an efficient alternative supply chain. However, it is untimely to imagine that they will cooperate to reach their aim faster: the rare earths market is too strategic to be split. In case either Russia or the United States finally start mining their minerals again, they will surely avoid sharing their new strategic assets.

A few months ago, a new "rare earths option" came out, which is linked to a new deposit found last July on the floor of the Pacific Ocean. The Japanese team which made the discovery argues that due to the heavy concentration of rare earths on this site, just one square kilometre of deposit will be able to provide one-fifth of the current global annual consumption. The minerals have been found in the sea mud extracted from depths of 3,500 to 6,000 metres below the ocean surface, in international waters, in an area stretching east and west of Hawaii, as well as east of Tahiti in French Polynesia. It has been estimated that the rare earths contained in the deposit amount to 80-100 billion metric tons, which is much more than the global reserves currently confirmed by the US Geological Survey.

The Japanese team clarified that extracting rare earths from this deposit requires pumping up materials from the ocean floor and that sea mud could be brought to ships and rare earths could be extracted later on using simple acid leaching. According to Japanese experts, the use of diluted acid, makes the process fast and it might take just a few hours to extract 80-90 per cent of minerals from the mud.

Despite that, the exploitation of this new huge rare earths site could be less easy than expected. Until now, no estimate of when extraction of the materials from the sea bed might start, has been provided. Before proceeding, it will be necessary on the one hand to better assess extraction costs and, on the other hand, clarify who has the right to access resources located in international waters. Even so, it is realistic to anticipate that in case sea mud extraction will not prove to be too expensive and time consuming, Japan, together with many other countries, will surely show an interest in securing rare earths imports from the new Pacific site.

Session II: Discussion

Issue Raised

The multiple multilateral mechanisms in the Asia Pacific today suffer from a lack of coordination. The oldest of them, the ASEAN increasingly focusses on issues of non-traditional security and preventive diplomacy. Will these frameworks balance the interests of both powerful and weak states to mitigate traditional security threats?

Responses

(a) There is indeed a need for a cohesive security framework, whose purpose and terms of reference need to be clear. The ASEAN Regional Forum, despite its shortcomings, is a very important platform for all countries to work together for mutual benefit.

(b) There is always benefit to be had in the creation of new mechanisms to address peace and security. The ARF so far is the most inclusive of the arrangements in the region and though it may be criticised as another talk shop, in international relations, it is always good to keep talking and have both bilateral and multilateral dialogues. The ARF could also be seen as a potential forum to address the South China Sea dispute.

Issue Raised

In 2007-2008 at an international conference on the environmental hazards of rare earth mining, it was decided that countries like India, Australia, the US and others would stop mining and close their mines till environment friendly options were arrived at. China too was a signatory to the agreement, but unlike other countries, it continues to flout its commitment and operates its mines. The WTO was approached over this breach but it failed to take any credible action. But the dependence on Chinese rare earth is likely to diminish by 2014. This is because the US and Australia both plan to reopen their mines in 2012 and India invests heavily in rare earth mining in countries like Madagascar, the Democratic Republic of Congo and Afghanistan.

Response

This information indeed brings to light the changing nature of mining of the rare earth scenario. One could hope for a time when the environment friendly options of the other countries would challenge Chinese hegemony in this area.

Issue Raised

The TPP has become a popular issue in academic and political circles, especially after endorsements by President Obama. What is Vietnam's take on Trans-Pacific Partnership?

Response

Vietnam sees TPP as a crucial link, with the US playing a leading role and regards it as the new potent factor in multilateral negotiations. It is unlikely that the TPP would replace the APEC, as it doesn't involve all members of the APEC. But it might, in the future, cause the economic disintegration of the ASEAN Member States.

Issue Raised

Within ASEAN, the TPP promises to act as a process towards regional integration and community building. What are the foreseeable pros and cons of the TPP?

Response

For Japan, the drive to join TPP is primarily economic. It has an ageing population and slowing economic growth and sees the TPP as an opportunity to leverage economic integration of the region. This, it feels, would contribute to the peace and stability of the region. Thus for Japan, joining the TPP is also a security strategy.

Issue Raised

The TPP and the EAS are the newest entrants in the already proliferating field of multilateral mechanisms in the Asia Pacific. The EAS has failed to deliver on all the expectations pinned on it. The consensus based nature of such institutions makes it difficult to arrive at rational decisions, making one less than hopeful. Has there been any assessment of the efficacy and the positives and negatives of such institutions?

Responses

(a) The idea of multilateralism, by nature, takes into account, national interests and community interests and thus is bound to make decisions haltingly. Though there are overlapping security mechanisms in the area which themselves are poorly linked and no objective assessment has been done as yet, the very fact that there has been relative peace and stability in the region speaks for itself. The APEC is an example of a successful institution that also helps keep peace in the region. In the future, the TPP and the APEC would compete and also complement each other for the benefit of the region.

(b) It is true that for institutions to work, good supporting spirit is essential. Perceptions with which parties enter into such institutions, whether they are realist or liberal, also matter. There is thus need for a larger broader vision and an appetite for mutual give-and-take. It is also possible to see the TPP as a strategic and political scheme, not so much economic.

(c) Seen from a perspective of the ecology of the international system, the proliferation of institutions is a general and expected phenomena, wherein Darwinian competition would ensure the survival of the most suitable institutions over time. Each of these institutions has contributed to the health of the region in their own ways. For example, the APEC had convinced the WTO to free the hold on IT products. Thus proliferation could result in competition and collaboration among institutions and this would only be in the interest of the region.

Issue Raised

Can we categorise aspirations of regional cohesion as 'must be', 'should be' or 'could be' achieved? There is a need for the assessment of regional institutions under these parameters.

Responses

(a) An assessment of the present and future during the session threw up areas for greater attention. The current peace that prevails in the region is very fragile; the security situation could worsen in a day's time, with adverse economic and security implications for most countries of the region. Therefore, with a focus on addressing asymmetry in power relations, there needs to be a continuous dialogue within the region.

(b) Economic frameworks in the region have lived up to regional aspirations. For all criticism of slow decision making, structures have endured. The region is today the economic powerhouse of the world. It is on the security front that much more needs to be done. At the same time it is unfair to expect regional frameworks to carry the burden of ensuring total security. The role of the US, the major powers and individual bilateral alliances would always be important. On the political front, the multilateral institutions have helped maintain confidence and gradually created a culture for countries to work together on numerous matters. This only bodes well for the future.

Issue Raised

How does one gauge the ASEAN and the ARF in leading the mantle of multilateralism in the region?

Response

The fifteen years of the existence of ARF has seen slow progress. It might not have lived up to its regional aspiration, but to discard it would be to expect too much. The ARF needs to be seen as a very loose institution, providing mainly a platform for dialogue. It has proved to be a confidence building mechanism for the region. This underscores the importance of the US to be involved in the region to provide public goods and to augment peace and stability, at both levels, bilateral and multilateral. As for the ASEAN, it is still in the driver's seat in the region, but requires the assistance of major powers of the region to keep playing an effective role.

Issue Raised

There is a huge presence of overseas Chinese in all significant areas in the region and the Chinese government actively engages them in the exercise of its soft power. What implications does this trend have for the region?

Response

Historically speaking, the Chinese population overseas hasn't had strong links with the mainland; they have been referred to as 'loose sand'. Their contribution has been most significantly towards the global supply chain.

Issue Raised

Regarding the nuclear weapons program of North Korea, where are the six party talks headed and what can be expected from it?

Response

There are divergent views on the intention of North Korea's nuclear program. One needs to consider that there have been historical instances where North Korea has considered denuclearisation, most notably in 1992. Thus there is hope. It might also be considered that aid could play a vital role in convincing North Korea to give up its program. The six party talks is in its seventh year now and all participants know each other better than before, many misperceptions and fears have been addressed. One can only be persevering and optimistic. Moreover, the talks are no longer only about the denuclearisation of North Korea, there is also a regional framework in the making. It has set itself new goals like the normalisation of relations between neighbours and increased cooperation for mutual prosperity.

Issue Raised

In light of the Spratly Islands dispute between China and Vietnam, what is China's reaction to Vietnam's request to India to explore natural resources in the area?

Response

Relations between Vietnam and China are improving. The Vietnamese Prime Ministers' visit to China in 2009 elicited positive responses. If China takes objection to the Indian exploration, Vietnam has appropriate answers ready. The Indian Ministry of Foreign Affairs is also abreast of the situation on a continuous basis.

Session II

Chairman's Concluding Remarks

Professor Richard Rigby (Australia)

We have been through a very fruitful afternoon, with much exchange of information and perspectives. No final conclusions are arrived at, but it is acknowledged that dialogue on all the issues discussed in the session must be continued. For an enduring regional architecture in the realms of economics and security we hope such dialogue is carried out in the spirit of transparency and sincerity of purpose on the part of all participants, with equality as the basis of mutual dealings.

SESSION III

BUILDING AN ENDURING SECURITY ARCHITECTURE FOR THE ASIA PACIFIC REGION

Auditorium

Chairman	-	Lieutenant General Vinay Shankar, PVSM, AVSM, VSM (Retd).
First Paper	-	Professor Su Hao, CFAU, China.
Second Paper	-	Professor Richard Rigby and Dr. Brendan Taylor, ANU, Australia.
Third Paper	-	Dr. Andrew C. Winner, NWC, USA.

Seminar Room 1

Chairman	-	Shri Ranjit Singh Kalha, IFS (Retd).
First Paper	-	Professor Swaran Singh, JNU.
Second Paper	-	Dr Kim Changsu, KIDA, South Korea.
Third Paper	-	Mr Fyodor Lukyanov, Editor-in-Chief, *Russia in Global Affairs*.

Discussion (In Auditorium)

Session III (Auditorium)
Chairman's Opening Remarks
Lieutenant General Vinay Shankar, PVSM, AVSM, VSM (Retd)

Let us begin with the presentations: we have Prof Su Hao from China speaking first. He shall talk about the concept of Integrative Security and Asia-Pacific Security Cooperation. Presenting an Australian point of view are Prof Richard Rigby and Dr Brendan Taylor. Finally Dr Andrew Winner will talk about Building an Enduring Security Architecture for the Asia-Pacific Region.

Session III

First Paper (Auditorium)

Professor Su Hao (China)

Concept of Integrative Security and Asia-Pacific Security Cooperation

My paper is centred on: a theoretical concept culled from traditional Chinese understanding and a new security concept.

The origin of the new security concept of the Chinese dates back to 1996. It differs from the official understanding on various scores. It builds primarily around mutual confidence, mutual benefit, the principle of equality and collaboration. It envisages a complex whole of Universal security, below which is common security, comprehensive security, then multilateral and cooperative security. The last two are the pillars of such an overall theory of security.

The concept of integrated security takes from traditional Han Chinese culture. It understands integration as a condition wherein many objects have been put together in an organic unity under a certain structural format. It envisages an organic continuum between the country, the region and the earth. Survival, then, is necessarily collaborative and realised within social institutions. Such an understanding is likely to promote the idea that China could be safe in a state of its neighbour's comfortableness.

The implication of such theory is that it would necessitate a process of integration. Since security is seen as an organic whole, with multiple systems and architectures interacting with one another within the whole, it would call for a regional integration for international order. This new regionalism or trans-regionalism could give way to open regionalism, along the ideas of frontiers in place of watertight borders. Therefore, an Asia Pacific Security

Cooperation, for China would be along a series, in continuum from local to global security structures. In the Asia Pacific region, there are presently lots of overlaps in the areas of trans regional cooperation, economic competition and institution-building, with the proliferation of Track 1, 2 and 3 initiatives.

Economic cooperation in the region is represented by the ASEAN and others. In the security field, there are the ARF, the CSCAP, the AD Roundtable, the Shangrila Dialogue, the ASEAN Security Community and others. These multiple initiatives have led to a structure like a bowl of spaghetti.

The larger and overarching framework of such interrelated initiatives is led by the two major powers, the US and China. The former is the pacific force, while the Asian side is led by China. Between the two, both have multiple bilateral, trilateral and multilateral relations with actors in the Asia-Pacific region. The structure so ensuing could be likened to a dumbbell. It reveals, however, the possibility of confrontation in the weaker middle. Therefore, efforts should be towards getting rid of individual military alliances in the future and to broaden the middle.

A final contribution of the paper would float the idea of the Biang-Biang model. Referring to a bowl of noodles, the idea of security so envisaged would hold diverse concepts like integrity and community together. Coming from such an understanding, there are several suggestions for regional security cooperation. They involve-

- The promotion of dialogue and coordination between different ideologies and social systems.
- The continued strengthening of Confidence Building Measures.
- In-depth discussion for preventive diplomacy etc.

The Asia Pacific region can be understood through its regional components of South East Asia, East Asia and North East Asia. The Pacific end of the region is typically US-centred and sees initiatives like the APEC, while the East is led by China and is realised in institutions like the East Asia Summit. We should be able to look at a 'dual core processor', a combination of the two ends, as a lasting and stable trans-Pacific Security Cooperation architecture.

Session III
Second Paper (Auditorium)

Dr Brendan Taylor and Professor Richard Rigby (Australia)

Recent years have seen a spate of new architectural initiatives proposed by governments in the Asia-Pacific region. Australia controversially advocated the building of an Asia-Pacific community by 2020, Japan suggested the construction of a slightly narrower 'East Asian community' which potentially excluded the United States, Indonesia posited the initially promising idea of establishing a G-8 grouping for Asia - which raised some concerns for the future of the Association of Southeast Asian Nations – to which Singapore replied with an ASEAN-plus-eight formula. However, none of these proposals have come to fruition, at least in the form in which they were originally proposed. Instead, the range of blueprints for Asia's emerging security architecture appear now to have settled around three more general approaches – 'exclusive regionalism', 'inclusive regionalism' and 'excluded regionalism.' This paper outlines and critically examines these three architectural approaches and offers tentative conclusions regarding which among the three will – and should – ultimately prevail.

The first 'exclusive regionalism' framework is ostensibly centred around ASEAN, but in reality is being driven by Beijing. Institutionally, it takes the form of the ASEAN-plus-three process – an organisation which is increasingly taking on a 'three-plus-ASEAN' character as a result of its annual trilateral summit comprising China, Japan and South Korea. Beijing's official rationale for championing this 'narrow regionalist' vision is a pragmatic one which suggests that meaningful cooperation becomes more achievable, the fewer the number of players involved. Much security cooperation between China and the ASEAN countries has thus far focussed upon the traditional security sector, where many, if not most Southeast Asian governments feel most comfortable, operating. Over time, however, this paper predicts that deepening economic and non-traditional security cooperation between China and ASEAN will conceivably also have strategic ramifications as it spills increasingly into more traditional forms of collaboration. The absence of the US from the 'exclusive regionalism' framework is significant from this perspective and highlights Beijing's underlying motivations in driving it forward.

The second 'inclusive regionalism' framework also pays lip service to ASEAN by assigning it a central position and institutionally takes the form of the East Asia Summit, as well as the newer ASEAN Defence Ministers' Meeting-Plus (ADMM+) gathering. This form of regionalism includes a number of countries not invited to participate in more exclusive groupings such as ASEAN-plus-three, including the United States, India, Australia, Russia and New Zealand. Officially, the rationale for including these players is that meaningful solutions to the raft of security challenges confronting the region during the so-called 'Asian century' cannot be arrived at unless Asia's great powers – the US, China, India, Japan and Russia – are involved. Unofficially, however, by including a larger number of players at the table, China's growing power and influence is able to be diffused more effectively in multilateral settings. This logic was certainly foremost in the minds of Japanese policymakers in 2005 when they worked assiduously to ensure that India, Australia and New Zealand became members of the fledgling East Asia Summit.

The third 'excluded regionalism' model is a direct 'hedge' on the part of those parties excluded under the first model and concerned that this first architectural blueprint might ultimately prevail. This particular architectural approach is predominantly US-centric in origin. It favours modes of security cooperation that are more ad hoc and functional in nature, although greater integration of the predominantly bilateral US-led Asian alliance network is often conceived as a basis for collaboration under this model. So-called 'minilateral' formats – such as the Trilateral Strategic Dialogue comprising the US, Japan and Australia - are also favoured over larger multilateral processes on the grounds that those parties with the greatest and most direct interest in a particular security problem or issue are also most likely to step forward to make meaningful contributions, thereby again circumventing the problem of achieving consensus that is so often seen to impede progress in multilateral settings.

The paper concludes with observations regarding the relationship between institutions and regional order more generally. Scholars of the Liberal persuasion argue that institutions play an integral role in shaping that order, whereas Realists suggest that the impact of institutions is marginal at best and tend more to reflect the prevailing order of the time. Whichever of these lines of argumentation one accepts, this paper contends that the best interests of India, Australia and, indeed, regional stability more generally would seem to lie with the second of the three models outlined. The paper will thus conclude by offering modest recommendations regarding what can be done to best advance the prospects for its prevailing.

Session III
Third Paper (Auditorium)

Dr Andrew C Winner (USA)

Building an Enduring Security Architecture for the Asia Pacific Region

In analytic as well as policy circles, discussions of security architectures often begin with questions of what type of international institution should be created or which states should be included or excluded. These are second order questions. The primary question is: what are the objectives of the architecture? What is the architecture supposed to accomplish?

In the Asia Pacific region and indeed in any regional formation, there are a range of potential goals for any security architecture. It should be understood that very ambitious objectives will decrease the possibility that such an architecture will be created, or even if it is created, if it will operate with any degree of efficiency or effectiveness. Less ambitious objectives increase the chances that such an architecture will both be formed, be effective and endure.

At the high end, security architecture can be meant to ensure peace and stability in the entire region or within certain sub-regions or dyads where conflict is deemed likely or particularly dangerous, were it to break out. The latter case might involve a situation where a crisis or conflict has the potential to escalate in one or more ways. One could be the likelihood that a conflict would draw in a larger number of states. Another would be that the conflict had the chance to escalate to the use of nuclear weapons or other types of warfare that could cause widespread loss of life or damage to infrastructure or economies. It may be that, due to their destructive capabilities, any security architecture in the Asia Pacific needs a place in it to address nuclear weapons and their possible use by states or non-state actors. In other words, a high end, ambitious goal would be prevention of conflict through some combination of deterrence, dissuasion and assurance.

The focus can be general – concern about any state-on-state threats or violence – or it can be specific. It could "name names" by identifying the state or states which are potentially problematic, or it could have more general objectives with regard to state-based security problems. One concept would be to protect states against rising states within the region, who had the potential to become hegemons. Determining which states are rising in the Asia Pacific is a relatively empirical exercise and likely could be done with little controversy. Agreeing on which of those rising states constitutes a potential hegemon, however, gets into the politically and diplomatically-fraught realm of perceptions. Another concept would be to focus on those states that have regularly violated norms of international behaviour or have had their actions formally designated as threats to international peace and stability through United Nations Security Council (UNSC) resolutions. An architecture could also be meant to ensure peace and stability in the region against threats from outside of the region – from a potential external aggressor or hegemon. If UNSC resolutions are a criteria or if the architecture is designed to deter or defend against an outside hegemon, it could raise questions about whether this is a regional architecture at all or whether this has essentially become something global.

An architecture designed to prevent intra-state wars could focus on collective defence, collective security, or some combination of the two. Collective defence would involve some types of formal commitments between or among states to take steps to deter and respond to aggression. Some bilateral and multilateral, formal, agreements of this sort already exist in the Asia Pacific region in the form of US treaties of alliance with Japan, the Republic of Korea and Australia/New Zealand. The five-power defence treaty involving the UK, Australia, New Zealand, Singapore and Malaysia, is another example of such a formal collective defence arrangement that already exists in the Asia Pacific region. An architecture with collective security elements would involve commitments, which could be legal and/or political, for all states to respond against any state-based threat or aggression.

Another possible objective would be to create a structure within which Asia Pacific states could cooperate more effectively to combat common security concerns, likely those of a transnational nature. This could involve creating cooperative elements designed to improve international response to natural disasters and humanitarian crises. It could involve a regional umbrella to improve cooperation to combat transnational terrorist groups, the proliferation of weapons of mass destruction, human trafficking, illegal fishing or smuggling.

A middle of the road, less ambitious goal for a security architecture would be not necessarily deter or defeat aggression by states but to reduce the chances that it might happen inadvertently or through the actions of the security dilemma. Such an architecture would emphasise increasing the predictability and transparency of security actions of major states. This could involve a range of elements that are often referred to as confidence building measures. In fact, a security architecture that emphasises prevention through individual or collective defence agreements and actions might require confidence building aspects in order to alleviate the potentially escalatory nature of self-help measures.

Recent experience in the Asia Pacific realm offers some evidence that the security dilemma operates, even in the absence of any agreement on formal collective defence agreements. China has fairly regularly objected to instances when the regular India-US annual naval exercise, Malabar, has been expanded to include other Asia Pacific nations. The recent Indian-Afghanistan strategic partnership agreement has increased concerns in Pakistan about encirclement and instability on that country's western border.

Another ambitious objective or set of objectives for a security architecture would be to decrease the chances of war or violence by addressing some of the potential causes of war or violence. As an example, if wars are sometimes fought over long-standing disputes involving borders or resources, security architecture could help decrease the chances for war if it helped to address or solve the historic or existing dispute. This could involve helping resolve border or boundary disputes that involve differing interpretations of international rights and obligations in the maritime domain.

An architecture of this sort implies that something would be put in place beyond bilateral negotiations or to assist bilateral negotiations among the parties to the existing dispute. A serious question for such an objective would be whether key Asia Pacific states would accept any sort of involvement in bilateral disputes. Key states to existing land and maritime border and boundary disputes, China and India, each have a preference for bilateral negotiations in these areas – each preferring to bring its significant bilateral political and economic weight to bear without the possibility of balancing behaviour that can occur in multilateral venues. Another potential challenge to architectures that look at root causes or long-standing disputes is that the issues quickly become closely related to internal questions of governance and justice. This quickly brings up questions of sovereignty and non-interference in internal affairs.

Another approach for a regional security architecture would be to leave the thorny questions of state-on-state violence and war to self-help and bilaterally-negotiated defence agreements and instead focus on combating transnational security issues such as terrorism, piracy, proliferation of weapons of mass destruction and trafficking in various potentially destabilising commodities such as narcotics or small arms and light weapons. Such a goal for a security architecture has two potential benefits in terms of achievability. One is that many of these issues threaten many states and cannot be solved unilaterally, so there are natural incentives to cooperate. A second order affect is that cooperation on these issues may ease the security dilemma by creating greater transparency and understanding of both capabilities and intentions. Such an objective, however, has potential problems as well. One is that of free-riding, where some states whose interests are threatened may choose to not participate in collective enterprises to address transnational issues, preferring instead to let others expend resources and themselves reap the security benefits. While this may work in the short-run, the question of burden-sharing may arise over time, potentially undermining cooperative efforts. Another issue is that many of the so-called transnational issues have direct connections to state policies and state security issues. Some terrorist groups are state-sponsored or are provided havens by states. Proliferation of weapons of mass destruction, while at times undertaken by or for non-state groups, is almost always in connection with a state-run weapons program. Trafficking in illegal or destabilising goods may be due to undergovernance or state policy in some states. A third issue that may have to be overcome is whether a transnational focus runs up against a global regime or architecture that is already in place to cover this issue. Can something like USNCR 1540, which focusses on the intersection of non-state actors and WMD, be implemented more effectively on a regional basis? How would a regional architecture with an objective of this type relate to the global mandate and regime?

As noted above, questions of geographic and/or membership scope are directly related to the objectives of the architecture. Given objectives, what is the geographic area that the architecture should cover and which states should it encompass? The Asia Pacific region is an amalgamation that allows a number of alternatives. One is to focus on the Asian landmass and security issues that connect it with the Pacific Ocean, or even more narrowly, to those that connect it to the western portion of the Pacific Ocean. A broader conception would include the Asian landmass as well as the two major oceans which border it – the Indian and the Pacific. A number of analytic organisations have already begun to take that approach in looking at future security considerations. In terms of maritime considerations, this makes eminent sense as oceans are highways with any meaningful borders other than chokepoints. Moreover, there is often substantial interaction between security issues on land and those in the maritime domain. The current example of this interaction is the piracy taking place off of Somalia. While the security issue occurs in the maritime domain, in particularly largely on the high seas, almost all governments and outside analysts agree that both its causes and solution, as opposed to just its partial mitigation, lie on land in Somalia.

Less clear is the question of what states could or should be included in any architecture. By what criteria should states be included: geography, economic interests, military capacity, political gravitas? Should there be criteria or preconditions for states to be included in any formal or informal arrangements that constitute an architecture? If so, what are those criteria, who sets them and how will it be determined whether a state has met the criteria or conditions? If one looks at an issue such as piracy off of the coast of Somalia, then it makes sense to include key states (and possibly international organisations such as the EU and NATO) from outside of the region that are contributing significantly in terms of diplomatic weight, economic resources, or military might. If the architecture is meant to address other state-on-state security issues within the region, then including outside actors may, or may not, be either necessary or helpful in terms of success.

As noted above, even if one has a very expansive conception of an Asian Pacific security architecture, in terms of both geography and participation, there is the question of how this architecture relates to the existing global security architecture or other regional structures. How related does an Asian Pacific structure have to be to the United Nations, to NATO and the European Union, to the African Union?

Security architectures are not constructed out of whole cloth. Any Asian Pacific architecture, regardless of objectives and scope, will have to involve, or at least take into account, existing elements that address security concerns. One obvious element is the set of existing bilateral, treaty-based, collective defence security relationships that the United States has with states in the Asia Pacific region. Another element is those sub regional groupings and organisations that already exist in the region such as ASEAN, the SAARC, the IOR-ARC and APEC. In addition, a range of less formal cooperative schemes exist in the region, such as the counter piracy patrols in the Gulf of Aden and Somali basin as well as global cooperative schemes with regional application, such as counter-proliferation efforts under the aegis of the Proliferation Security Initiative. Existing relationships, organisations and efforts can also gain new missions, increase or decrease in emphasis or be repurposed under a new architecture – assuming, of course, that the members or participants in those existing forums agree to those changes.

Similarly, security architectures do not have to be fully developed or fully defined at their outset. The objectives of the architecture do not have to be shared by all of those who might be involved or affected by elements of the architecture. The goals, scope and participants can change over time. Long-lasting and effective architectures tend to be flexible. They can start small and become more ambitious, or they can identify a very ambitious need and be created to address it. This is in part the diplomatic art of any such enterprise and it is the skill of those who implement it. However; flexibility also has to be considered in the design phase. Otherwise, diplomats, politicians and military officers will find themselves constantly searching for something new rather than building on existing arrangements, organisations and patterns and habits of interaction.

Session III (Seminar Room 1)
Chairman's Opening Remarks

Shri Ranjit Singh Kalha, IFS (Retd)

The topic, as you all know, is 'Building an Enduring Security Architecture for the Asia Pacific Region'. We have three panelists presenting their papers and if I may go by the order that is indicated here, the first speaker will be Professor Swaran Singh.

Professor Swaran Singh teaches Diplomacy and Disarmament Studies at the Centre for International Politics, Organisation and Disarmament in the School of International Studies, Jawaharlal Nehru University. He is the President of the Association of Asian Scholars - an Asia wide network with its Secretariat in Delhi. He is the General Secretary of the Indian Association of Asian and Pacific Studies and Bangkok based Asian Scholarship Foundation's Regional Review Committee for South Asia.

Professor Singh has travelled and written extensively on Asian Affairs, China's Foreign and Security Policy Issues with special focus on China-India Confidence Building Measures, as also on Arms Control and Disarmament, Peace and Conflict Resolution, India's Foreign and Security Policy Issues. Professor Singh has authored 'India-China Economic Engagement: Building Mutual Confidence', 'China-South Asia: Issues, Equations, Policies' and 'China's Changing National Security Doctrines and Limited War'. He has also edited the 'China-Pakistan Strategic Cooperation: Indian Perspectives' and co-authored 'Regionalism in South Asian Diplomacy'. I now give the floor to Professor Swaran Singh to make his presentation.

Session III
First Paper (Seminar Room 1)

Professor Swaran Singh

Security Architecture in The Asia-Pacific

If you look at the conference brochure with the outline of today's program, you would find a map of the Asia-Pacific region at its back cover. I would suggest that you take a look at the map at some point; it would give you a lot of ideas about what the organisers wish to convey to participants of this conference. A picture says a thousand words as they say; and the map could be an useful starting point for us to get a grip on where we are and where we are going. What I am trying to underline here is that India, as we know, has become an integral part of the Asia-Pacific region.

Secondly, I enjoyed listening to several eminent speakers yesterday and today morning. I was especially looking forward to hearing some presentation or discussion on security 'architecture' in the Asia-Pacific region. But this so-fashionable expression, 'architecture', has escaped the stand-alone scrutiny that I think is required of it. While we discussed in detail all the aspects and issues that form an integral part of emerging security architecture, there is still space for me to dwell on the subject of what do we wish to portray when we speak about security 'architecture' for the Asia-Pacific region. Of course there are several components, several perspectives, on this 'architecture' which are individually extremely important for evolving canvass; but then the big picture of what constitutes this security 'architecture' is also equally important. This is the question that I wish to address as I begin my presentation.

While contemplating to participate in today's panel discussion, I began looking for answers to the questions of what do we mean by architecture? We seem to adapt this expression into our deliberation without required auditing of this formulation. Wherefrom has this expression evolved or how have we borrowed it into discourses of international relations? At the very outset, it is important to underline that just like all other critical issues, perspectives, theories, map-making that engage our attention and guide our lives, semantics also remain politically value-loaded and politically-driven. Sometimes these semantics circumscribe and narrow down our options to conceive of various alternative paradigms in discourses. If we are popularising this expression of security 'architecture', are we at least in the know of and comfortable with this expression as the guiding axiom of this conference's explorations? What do we mean by 'architecture' is perhaps the first question that we need to address.

What is Architecture?

The first classic on 'architecture' was written by an ancient Greek philosopher, Vitruvius and it has survived to be the guiding holy book for modern architects and other disciplines that owe to architecture. The book is titled as *De Architectura*. For Vitruvius, architecture was defined by its three famous pillars: durability, utility and beauty. These three elements formed the basis behind the idea of Greek architecture that has produced several historic structures. These structures both reflected and directed the social and political discourses and ways of life. For example, this was the time of civilizational dominance, when ancient civilizations laid emphasis on discourses amongst its 'citizens' as way of ensuring control of human life of plebeians on planet earth.

The story of 'architecture' was to move from there and undergo a major transformation through modern ages and its new watersheds like mercantilism, Protestantism, Industrial Revolution, which were to unleash an era of imperialism and nationalism and the ideas of liberty, equality, justice were developed further. For instance, the centrality of the sovereign was drifting to aristocracies and even masses and the sovereign personified by the King or the Emperor had to reinforce mandate of heavens and aggrandize his charisma. This was sought to be done by maximizing 'power' through recruiting mass armies and mass production of weapons as also by emphasising on their grandeur through 'architecture' that symbolised the sovereign.

In the age of machines and technology, debates on 'architecture' were to witness a second famous book on architecture being published in year 1894. This was written by famous art critic of Great Britain, John Ruskin and was titled as *Several Lands of Architecture*. It was written in the wake of rising British Empire and the transformation in the basic meaning of 'architecture' was noticeable. Ruskin believed that the architecture was an "art that so adorns edifices raised by men...that the sight of them contributes to mental health, pleasure and power" which was way apart from original axioms of durability, utility and beauty of Greek philosopher, Vitruvius. The pomp and glory was writ-large on these new connotations of 'architecture' discourse. Power was the most defining feature of architecture under European imperialists and this has been the most dominant notion that we have inherited in our discourses on international relations.

Towards the end of the 20th century, the idea of security architecture was first developed in Information Technology sector; just as fusion and fission in Nuclear Physics was borrowed from Biology to explain what nuclear scientists had discovered. So, what did 'security architecture' mean in the domain of Information Technology? This not only meant ensuring availability of data but also ensuring confidentiality and integrity of data processed. Are these elements central to security architecture in international relations or for security in the Asia Pacific region? So, as we debate the security architecture for Asia-Pacific, are we discoursing evolution of such power-driven structures? While the 21st century world has clearly moved from power-driven multipolar or bipolar world of cold war years to norms and institutions-driven multilateralism, we may be misled by such semantics like architecture. Community building, for instance, could be our alternative paradigm! This will make it possible for us to look beyond the box.

Security Architecture in the Asia-Pacific

Among various scholars that I admire are William Toe and Brandon Taylor. They wrote an interesting article in 2010 in the *Review of International Studies* exploring this questions of "What is Asia's Security Architecture?"

which was the title of their paper. They came to the conclusion that the Asia-Pacific region was experiencing multiple discourses, multiple connotations and multiple perspectives within these discourses on the subject of their security architecture. In fact, they identified this multiplicity as the basic anomaly and basic lacuna in these discourses not being able to deliver any pan-Asia-Pacific security structures. This was a reflection of the lack of singular vision and blueprint for the region and there is no clear conception of security architecture for the Asia Pacific.

Ron Huisken, who authored a book titled *The Architecture of Security in Asia-Pacific* that was published in 2009, is more optimistic. He does not rule out the possibilities of some kind of pan-Asia-Pacific formulations emerging sometime in the future. Indeed he sees this as likelihood around the core of Association of South East Asian Nations (ASEAN) which has lately introduced various multilateral forums involving major powers from across the Asia-Pacific region. Ron sees this reality of ASEAN emerging at the driving seat as a result of continuing ambivalence amongst major regional powers on (i) who should become the sculptor of such security architecture and (ii) what should be the character of such structure or structures. It is in such ambivalence that ASEAN emerged as agreeable convener of such efforts but, understandably, ASEAN functions under the severe restraint of not ever hurting the core national interest of any of these major players. This means that while there is hope, it may still take a long time to materialise.

I assume that the challenge for a conference like this one is to ask not only what do we mean by security architecture but also to interrogate what are the reasons for this multiplicity of ideas and experiments as also whether such a multiplicity can be treated as the essential nature of security architecture in the Asia-Pacific. After all, security architecture of this region does not have to necessarily resemble other models and examples. I particularly enjoyed listening to Dr. Chan's presentation from Taiwan yesterday when she spoke of the need for balancing the body, mind and soul in regional security architectures. I think we should focus on that triadic nature to understand what appear to be disjunctions between how the Asia-

Pacific thinks about its security architecture through its tradition, indigenous wisdom and culture; and structures that we inherited from our colonial masters. There is perhaps need to reconcile or fine-tune these disjunctions.

I particularly enjoyed Bharat Karnad's formulation yesterday which also reflected similar sentiments, emphasising value of ensuring "organic evolution of Asian perspective" which does not have to be exclusive but where the core focus must be *Asian* wisdom or a set of core of Asian perspectives or traditions. All of you might remember the Secretary General of ASEAN, Rodolfo Severino. He wrote a book titled *South East Asia in Search of ASEAN Community* that was published in the year 2006. In this he had also underlined the fact as to how the ASEAN-centric initiatives owe their origins not to the Cold-War dynamics as this has been generally understood in popular literature on this subject. He has highlighted common Asian traditions. In this context, there have been allusions to the Asian Relations Conference that took place in New Delhi in March-April 1947, several months before India's independence. Secretary Severino also talks of the Afro-Asian Bandung Conference as a precursor of the Association of Asian Countries of 1961 which was soon replaced by ASEAN in 1967 as drawing inspirations from Asian traditions.

It is interesting to note that the ASEAN, which is seen at the core of regional initiatives to evolve a new security architecture, in its Charter Article 1, underlines how they will work to "enhance peace, security and stability" in the region. I always like to underline that unlike the Occident that sees peace in security, the Orient sees security in peace. Asian traditions privilege peace over security. This makes approaches to security in Asia-Pacific at variance to the dominant discourses on security management in the Western world. This decides how security architecture in Asia-Pacific will take shape and what will be effective for this region. In the post-Cold War world, the first attempt at security at the Asia-Pacific level was pushed by the ASEAN and took shape in the form of the Asian Regional Forum (ARF). But it is interesting to note that the guiding axiom in the concept note of ARF did not have the word security. Instead it emphasised "peace and prosperity" as its main objectives. Privileging peace over security again clearly comes across in this conception – if you have peace, indeed, you have security!

And in ARF, this focus on peace and prosperity in Asia-Pacific was expected to be achieved using three steps for promoting confidence building measures, by promoting preventive diplomacy and by developing conflict resolution mechanisms. If these were to be their mechanisms then the long-term goals of this ARF security architecture were defined as the Security Community, the Economic Community and the Socio-cultural Community. Are we at home with these techniques and these goals? ARF was launched in 1994; but what we forget is equally interesting and effective security architecture, called the Shanghai Five, was to be launched just two years later. From 2001, it was to take the form of the Shanghai Cooperation Organisation (SCO). This forum has undergone major transformations in the last twenty years as has since emerged as a successful model of regional security.

One could likewise talk of the South Asian Association for Regional Cooperation and many others. Indeed, the Asia-Pacific region can boast of several successful forums and structures that have become effective tools for ensuring security in various sub-regions of the Asia-Pacific region. But it is important to note that most of them have lately also evolved pan-Asian-Pacific consciousness and this has witnessed change in the nature of their participants and agendas. Most of these forums have now begun to involve participants from other parts of the Asia-Pacific region as observers, dialogue partners or just as special invitees. This again speaks of their indigenisation and evolution of security architecture that may be better rooted in the local traditions of the Asia-Pacific region.

Shifting Sands of Time

In more specific terms, the story of the evolution of contemporary security architectures in Asia-Pacific region goes back to the US withdrawal from Subic Bay in the Philippines, followed by the Soviet withdrawal from Cam Rahn Bay in Vietnam. These were part of events that heralded the beginning of the end of the Cold War rigid bipolar system and created spaces in the Asia-Pacific for local initiatives, both for ensuring their security and development. But more than this, it also gradually highlighted how this process had also triggered change in nature of tools and strategies, of how these new actors were to approach these issues and evolve new paradigms or evolved their existing structures.

The US, for instance, has had its major focus on military means as preferred tools for ensuring security across this region. Accordingly, the security architecture of Asia-Pacific had been built by the US had been one of the hub-and-spokes of its military alliances and military arrangements or defence cooperation with various countries of the Asia-Pacific region. But in the last twenty years, China has risen as a major influence yet it has not replicated any hub-and-spokes system of military alliances and its 'ways' do not necessarily follow cold war formulations. China has gradually used its economic engagements and soft-power and moved from being a norm taker to being a norm maker, or so it aspires. In fact, the economic growth of countries like Vietnam, Indonesia, Malaysia, India, Australia and many more together marks the rise of the Asia-Pacific region.

But the rise of China has also created disjunctions as it seeks to recast the regional order. One can notice a kind of division of labour emerging between the United States and China. While US continues to focus on military security, China focusses on economic security. This glaring disjunction at the face has made the US leadership realise the role of economic security as well. Therefore, the US is now trying to wind up its military operations in Iraq and Afghanistan. Secretary of State, Hillary Clinton, has been talking of new foreign policy reorientation based on the triad of diplomacy, development and defence. This seems better tuned with Asia-Pacific region where diplomacy and defence have always been viewed as two sides of the same coin, working in tandem with each other.

Implications for India

Finally, debates of this nature in New Delhi naturally draw attention to what all these things mean for India. More than working in tandem, India has always favoured diplomacy over defence. In recent times, India has been an integral part of most new multilateral initiatives in the Asia-Pacific region with East Asian Summits being the most recent example. India is now more welcome and she has emerged as more visible. Of course, there is an urgent need for India to set its home in order. But the juncture where India now stands has been unusual in its history. For the first time in its history, all major powers have comfortable relations with India.

Secondly, India has always been extremely comfortable with the idea of multilateralism. We are a mosaic society and we have always argued in favour of several multilateral fora. Besides, India is increasingly seen not only as a source of ancient wisdom but also of material help. We started ITEC and now we can see India helping many East Asian countries like Cambodia or Vietnam. Multiple arrangement is something that does not come across as an aberration to us. Diversity is natural to Asia. In the future, multilateralism will be the norm instead of an exception. As a large society, India has successfully managed a democratic system with its vision of "unity in diversity". That is something that India will take to Asia.

SAARC too, is beginning to grow in pan-Asia-Pacific consciousness and participation and is gaining respectability and acceptance. As a result, SAARC has US, China, Japan and South Korea – major Asia-Pacific powers – as Observers. South Asia and South East Asia are coming closer. This naturally creates better external environment for India to play a greater role in the Asia-Pacific region. It is in this positive framework that India has to articulate its vision and to explore commonalities that it shares with other similar visions across the Asia-Pacific region. And it is in this enterprise of sculpting the organic security architecture for regional security that fine tuning the equilibriums amongst body, mind and soul of Asia-Pacific needs to be addressed.

Session III
Second Paper (Seminar Room 1)

Dr Kim Changsu (South Korea)

My focus will be on North East Asia because our concern has been North and South Korea, Japan and Vietnam, in Asia. My approach is step by step from one level to another- from the local to the regional. We are not a global country, our focus is on the region. I think our common interests are economic growth, stability, democratisation, deterrence of all-out wars, securing oil and natural resources, nonproliferation, counter-proliferation, nuclear terrorism, climate change and so on.

The major concerns, of course, are China's rise to the second largest economy and its growing in significance and influence. US-China relations also remain the most significant factor in global and security dynamics. Rebalancing US-Japan relations, including their postures towards economic power and military modernisation, relocation of US troops and facilities are other causes of concern. The increasing prominence of the BRICs, especially, India and its implications for regional security is another challenge. Crisis management and peace-building remain a big concern, including the possible integration and unification of the two Koreas. Competition for the Global Commons, conflict of national interests and the lingering threat of proliferation of WMDs and missiles are some more challenges. Other challenges include counterterrorism in Afghanistan, Iraq and other countries, transnational threats, natural disasters, energy and water shortages et al.

Obstacles exist primarily due to conflicting national interests and different visions for the future. However, in terms of regional cooperative mechanisms, Korean activities and interests include APEC, ARF, ASEAN and East Asia Summit, IISS Asia Security Summit, NEACD, the Beijing Six-Party Talks on North Korean nuclear issue and other Asia Pacific regional security mechanisms.

We advocate an alliance to ensure a peaceful, secure and prosperous future for the Korean Peninsula and welcome a comprehensive strategic alliance of bilateral, regional and global scope, based on common values and mutual trust.

For increased regional cooperation, it is also important to respond to various global security challenges of terrorism, proliferation of WMDs, piracy, drug and human trafficking, natural and man-made disasters, climate change and energy shortage. It is as significant to use existing and emerging multilateral mechanisms such as NPT, IAEA, MTCR, WA, HCOC, PCI, APEC, OECD/ DAC, NSS and G20.

There should be an end to the division of the Korean peninsula through peaceful means. This requires that the existing armistice agreement be replaced with a new peace treaty, implementation of political and military CBMs and arms control measures and the formulation of a peaceful unification formula in a manner acceptable to the neighbouring countries.

There is a need to deter DPRK's nuclear weapons and missile threat. Therefore, the US should provide extended deterrence, including nuclear umbrella, conventional strike capabilities and missile defence and Beijing Six-Party Talks must continue, apart from engaging other regional powers and multilateral mechanisms towards this end.

Therefore, enduring regional security architecture in the Asia Pacific should be built on tackling various regional security issues, both traditional and non-traditional, through a minimalist approach. A different group of bilateral, trilateral and other multilateral cooperation can coexist and should not be viewed as conflicting with each other. The North Korean nuclear weapons issue also must be handled at several international forums and dialogues for the benefit of entire East Asia. An enduring regional security architecture in the Asia Pacific thus requires multilateral security dialogues and cooperative mechanisms.

Session III
Third Paper (Seminar Room 1)

Mr. Fyodor Lukyanov

So far, the Asia Pacific has not been the centre of Russian foreign policy debate. It must also be interesting for all present here to start to learn what Russia is trying to do in order to become a part of Asian politics. The common sense in Russia is that there is a vacuum in the security field in Asia and that Asia should learn from Europe. I do not think this approach is true. The Russian approach is different.

Actually, the Russian turn toward Asia started after the Cold War and ended with the fall of the Soviet Union. The main axis of Russian foreign policy after the Cold War had been overwhelmingly West-centric. We had pro-Western theories in the beginning. Russian foreign policy has been determined by the willingness to root for the West, which was seen as the victor of the Cold War, to prove that Russia was still at the centre of the world even after the collapse of the Soviet Union. In other words, the two reference points of Russian foreign policy have been-one, the collapse of the Soviet Union and two, to convince and prove to the West that we are still here. That started to change quite recently because now it is obvious that the post-Soviet agenda with the two reference points have been exhausted. In a month, we are going to formally remember 20 years of the collapse of the Soviet Union. Russian mentality has started to change. It is going through the process that many empires go through in Europe-the "logic of non-empire". Russia has started to shift towards new issues and challenges in Asia.

Russia is unique in its position. It is European in mentality but 77 per cent of its territory is in Asia. People in Russia do not realise that three quarters of Russian territory is not in Europe. The shift towards Asia has happened thanks to President Medvedev. In him, the West sees a supporter but that is a paradox. It was Putin who was more pro-West, although the West thought that he was hostile to it. President Medvedev just smiles more than Putin! President Medvedev himself is important; like President Obama who is the first non-European to become the American President, President Medvedevalso is the first non-European Russian President.

The major task for Russian foreign policy and strategy is to formulate comprehensive means on a number of issues regarding Asia. It should develop strategies about how to develop the Siberian far East which is sparsely populated and how to participate in the Asia Pacific for years to come which is going to become the centre of international affairs. From the point of view of geopolitics, Russia is not an Asian country. How does Russia understand security in the Asia Pacific? Russia has almost exclusively focussed on China. This is understandable, considering it is Russia's biggest neighbour and has been rising continuously. Russia is concerned about how China will be in twenty years' time or fifty years' time. Looking at China, in Russia you will find several opinions from panic attacks to arguments that China should be the only natural partner in Asia because in a future world order China will be extremely powerful and it is in Russia's interest to cultivate China. In President Medvedev's discourse about Asia and China, we see a couple of problematic statements. He was the first to introduce the modernisation debate in Asia. Traditionally, Russia has only focussed on the West, in its belief that it was Europe which was modern and developed. But in a profound shift of Russian mentality, we have come to admit that many of the countries to Russia's east are more developed than Russia in terms of technology, level of relation etc.. This has been a revelation for Russia, because as a former colonial power, Russia has looked at China with some degree of superiority. This is no longer the case. There are debates about how Russia and China could cooperate more, at the same time also how not to become completely dependent on China.

The main point of debate in geopolitics is whether Russia becomes the bargaining chip, in the risk, in a hypothetical confrontation between China and United States. There are different opinions on that question. One opinion is that it will be of extreme advantage to Russia to be able to become the kingmaker. But in order to become a kingmaker one needs extremely well-calculated and smart policies, which frankly, Russia does not show very regularly. So, another opinion is that Russia will be a hostage to this situation. Hostility between the two countries will be extremely damaging for Russia. What is essential in Russia's case is that unlike Europe, Russia and US still see each other as opponents, despite the end of the Cold War. We might say a lot of beautiful words but the game is zero- sum. In Asia, the situation is different. In Asia, it is possible for Russia and US to cooperate because of the rise of China, tremendous shift in geopolitical contexts and because it has not been a traditional region for Russia and US to contest. Because of this, many believe that Russia needs to secure its military presence in the Asia Pacific. The formal explanation is Japan and that it needs to secure its territory from Japan. But Russia needs to show its symbolic presence through this. In Russia's perception, this region is of extreme importance.

Russia states officially that there is need for diversification in Asia. In this, India is our primary partner. Russia gives extreme importance to South Korea and also Japan, although with Japan we have our territorial issues. Finally, I would mention the North Korean issue because I think that it is probably the only region of conflict where Russia can play an important role. First of all, that is because Russia occupies a unique status in this conflict. Russia is more or less on friendly terms with all parties to the conflict. Recent attempt to offer a new paradigm of resolution of conflict through economically engaging North Korea could be productive by providing a new framework to resolve the issue. Russia's hydrocarbon potential could serve a useful means in this case to offer something new and get North Korea out of complete self-seclusion. Finally, there is a growing consensus in Russia that without serious engagement with South Asia and Asia Pacific, Russia has no chance of remaining significant in the 21st century because the situation has changed. Russia has to concentrate on Asia.

Session III: Discussion

Issues Raised

The seminar invites criticisms on two counts; firstly, a theoretical mistake- Is there one example in human history, where security architecture has ensured peace? It seems to be a silly idea and theoretically wrong. Henry Kissinger, in his recent book, 'On China', vindicates the same. It would be a more fruitful enterprise to find and interrogate the factors that cause war in Asia and how to avoid the same.

Secondly, for all the focus on regional actors, the conference has tended to miss the importance of the Sino-US relationship that is the single most decisive factor for peace in the region. There is a joint US-China security architecture in the making, wherein every year, half of the Cabinets of both countries meet and interact on issues ranging from commerce to defence and the economy. The deliberations might be secretive, but are far reaching in their implications. History too has it that the Cold War relations between the US and China focussed on 35 Asian countries and their architecture. The conference made no mention of it in the two days.

Responses

(a) No one denies the importance of the Sino-US bilateral relations for security and stability of the Asia Pacific region, but the conference, on part of the Australians was an effort to think out of the box. Moreover, a case can be made that security architecture exists. It is built on what States do to achieve their security. The effort should be to focus on its essential elements.

(b) The reminder that US and China are on the same boat more extensively than is assumed is often criticised within India. But events have borne out this fact. Time and again, the US has taken the side of China in any dispute with India. Also, the profile the US and Chinese armed forces do not indicate a clash; the US is a naval power, while China is primarily a land power.

(c) Security Architectures of the past have usually been the result of war and the imposition of the victor's idea of security. Currently the attempt is to arrive at an inclusive architecture in the absence of war. The importance of the Sino-US relations are not being discounted, it is also known that between the two, there were plans to manage South Asia. At the same time, the fissures between the two are also known. The G2 for instance is more keenly pursued by the US than China. The seminar could at least bring up issues and concerns raised by other countries of the region, the real stakeholders that should be taken up for consideration by China and the US in their private deliberations.

(d) Regarding the success of security architectures, the EU stands as a current example. Following the legacy of the World Wars, a process of integration had been doggedly pursued. The NATO, the EU all contributed to a complex architecture. EU is aware and approves of the large-scale bilateral discussions between the US and China, but believes that it is not an isolated phenomena. The EU has a similar structure of consultation with the Chinese. There is no monopoly of such interactions. The seminar has addressed some very relevant issues in a desirable manner.

(e) A condominium approach to manage the world is feasible only in theory; in reality inclusiveness and equal stakes of all actors are factors that can't be avoided. The G2 has its own merits and dangers, if it were as sustainable as was projected, there would have been many alternate outcomes to world events by now. Therefore, a seminar like this, seeking to address aspirations and concerns of all regional actors has potency.

(f) The international system has changed a lot in the last few decades and is beyond the domination of only two great powers, namely the

US and China. While the US has shrunk in power and spread, China is undergoing massive transformations itself. There is massive scope for other countries to contribute to lasting security in the region. The intention of such an attempt would be not to exclude the US-China factor but to complement it.

(g) One is reminded of Morgenthau's insight that the international scenario is always in flux; by the time foreign policy is conceived and put to motion, the world seems to change. In the past, security architectures have not worked because they were one sided and post war efforts, they were the victor's architecture. The idea of security community as imagined by Karl Deutsch has great currency for our circumstances. A non-American understanding of international relations is more comfortable with the idea of frontiers rather than borders. Thus, to evolve an effective architecture, there might not be need to integrate state sovereignty but work in spite of it. In Asia, we have used peace to ensure security, rather than security to achieve peace, but it is a difficult idea to translate because of the fundamental difference in semantics with western concept. It is, therefore, a commendable effort that the seminar is geared towards.

Issue Raised

How does one apply the Chinese logic of international relations to Western IR of the Westphalian legacy? Talking of an internal Chinese logic takes away from the urgency of dealing with current issues with a world bred in Western IR.

Response

There is no doubt that the West dominates our epistemic and discursive imagination. The nation-state itself is a western concept. But the world today has evolved to something beyond a Westphalian system. It is not enough to only manage one's own challenges. It is time that attention was paid to the oriental understandings of western concepts like sovereignty as conflicts in this region are often led on by actors with an oriental understanding of western IR. One feels, for instance that Westphalian notion of sovereignty is not the appropriate way to deal with the dispute of the South China Sea. There is a case to be made for a BlueOcean strategy.

Issue Raised

The Chinese understanding of international relations spoke of modest goals, whereas the Seminar envisages security and stability across a huge geographical expanse. Is it desirable to approach questions of peace and security through overarching institutions or through smaller economic and political structures that are localised in nature?

Response

Any enduring security architecture would have to be a combination of both modest localised concerns as well as overarching in scope. A two level model for that could be likened to a walnut. The outer hard shell refers to an overarching architecture like the EAS, but without the fruit, i.e. the regional powers and their interrelations, there would be no meaning to the shell. The SCO is another example of trying to manage regional security concerns through smaller, localised cooperation.

Issue Raised

In the conception of China as the custodian of an overarching security architecture for the Asia-Pacific region, there is cause for concern regarding elements within the PLA. Will China be able to manage its own sections that harbour a more hawkish and less inclusive idea of security?

Response

The two levels of security architecture envisage a dialectical relationship. The presence of US and other big powers fares well for East Asia as a whole. The more important challenge for China, one would think, would be on how to manage relations between the outer layer of world powers and the inner layer of the regional actors. Therefore, both China's multilateral and bilateral engagements are equally important.

Issue Raised

Any security architecture manages only to delay the occurrence of war and not prevent it altogether. How much merit is there in the idea of creating zones of neutrality with adequate defences, like that of the Swiss in the Second World War?

Responses

(a) The efficacy of a security architecture also depends on its structure- whether it is top-down or bottom-up. An architecture by itself does not guarantee even a delay in the occurrence of war. We are used to only certain kinds of architecture as of now. Maybe in the future, security architectures will be bottom up and thus more lasting. Also, most solutions in international relations only manage to delay violence. No human creation guarantees the total absence of war.

(b) While considering an alternate imagination of architectures, it is also advisable to look at the EU. War between Germany and France is unthinkable in current times. Therefore, architectures are only as good as its constituents make them.

Session III (Auditorium)
Chairman's Concluding Remarks

Lieutenant General Vinay Shankar, PVSM, AVSM, VSM (Retd)

Director of the USI, Lieutenant General PK Singh and Professor Swaran Singh have already commented on the reservations of Dr Michael Pillsbury. In cricketing terms, I will call what he threw at us, a googly. Speaking on behalf of the USI, I wish he had raised this issue before we began rather than at the concluding stage of the event. He has indeed raised a fundamental question – the compatibility of peace and security in any architecture. It deserves a separate seminar of its own. But I do believe that it is possible to locate peace and security in a single package, in any case, that is where mankind should be looking.

For my next observation, I am very grateful for the idea raised by Lieutenant General Tran Thai Binh and Lieutenant General Bang Hyo-Bok in the morning. Two Generals stating that nations should abjure the use of force sends a very good message to the Asian community and the larger world. To that I would add a third and speak on behalf of the Indian uniformed community present among the audience. All nations should work towards abjuring the use of force.

My third observation is on the ASEAN; I don't think we recognise adequately the significance of the achievements that the founding fathers of the organisation have contributed. Set up in 1967 with just six countries, apart from 1979, the region, till date, has witnessed no serious interstate conflict. It has grown in prosperity and security has prevailed. There was a hiccup in the 1990s, with the financial crisis, otherwise, ASEAN has reflected the dynamism to evolve and move on by creating additional fora like the ARF and now the EAS. I agree with some of the speakers that we need to set store and have faith in this organisation and its derivatives. It has contributed a lot to the region and has set a good example. No organisations or structures are perfect, but the founding ASEAN and its derivatives need to be commended.

Lastly, I would like to take note of a more serious issue-that of the spread of nuclear weapons. Two papers were presented on the subject yesterday. In one we spoke about the absence of moral authority amongst the nuclear weapons states to impose the NPT and the CTBT on everyone else. Therefore, this issue needs some looking into again. Related to this, was the point made by Professor Bharat Karnad- the imminence, possibility or rationale of these weapons spreading. How Japan has a genuine reason to go nuclear. South Korea and Vietnam should look at it.

One doesn't need a risk manager to remind them that as these weapons spread legitimately, the danger of them being used, spreads exponentially and there is a great cost for the entire human race. I think a forum like this should raise this issue with all the seriousness and urgency that this matter deserves. There is a case for calling for total nuclear disarmament, a weapons free world, implemented in a time bound manner and as soon as possible. Otherwise no one can promise that mankind would remain safe and prosper.

VALEDICTORY SESSION

Valedictory Address - Shri Ranjan Mathai, IFS, Foreign Secretary.

Vote of Thanks - Lieutenant General PK Singh, PVSM, AVSM (Retd), Director, USI.

VALEDICTORY ADDRESS
Shri Ranjan Mathai, IFS, Foreign Secretary
(Read by Ambassador AK Mukerji, IFS, Additional Secretary, MEA)

Over the past two days, you have discussed the broad aspects of peace and security in the Asia Pacific region. This includes its strategic and security dimensions, its political and economic frameworks, as well as the ongoing efforts to build an enduring security architecture for the region.

We are currently witnessing a historical shift in economic power towards Asia. Most commentators predict that the 21st Century will be an Asian Century. Led by the fast-paced and historic rise of China which has experienced growth rates averaging some 10 per cent per annum over three decades, Asia is home to some of the most rapidly growing economies of the world. The rise, over these past years, of Asian supply chains have integrated the region into a dynamic economic continuum, ranging from the more advanced countries of East Asia such as Japan and South Korea through the so-called "newly industrialised" economies of Singapore, Malaysia and Taiwan to the more recent dynamo economies such as Indonesia, Vietnam and India. Intra-regional trade and investment flows are rising rapidly, binding the countries of this region ever closer together.

India's engagement with the Asia Pacific region has focussed primarily on our engagement with South East and East Asia. We articulated our 'Look East' policy twenty years ago. It is a geographical fact that India is in the immediate neighbourhood of several of the countries of the Association of South-East Asian Nations (ASEAN). We share land and maritime borders with Myanmar, Indonesia and Thailand, less than 150 kilometres separate, the Indian island of Nicobar from Sumatra in Indonesia. We see ourselves as much as an East Asian as a South Asian country – in terms of our geography, historic connections and economic linkages.

We believe that the countries of the Asia Pacific region now recognise the impact of India's socio-economic transformation on the reshaping of the global economic order. India's continued economic growth, averaging 7-8 per cent per year, also provides significant opportunities for accelerating Asia's own growth. The importance of ensuring this through specific structures of bilateral and regional cooperation between India and the countries of the Asia Pacific region is, therefore, self-evident.

India's linkages with the Asia Pacific region are anchored in the maritime lanes of the Indian Ocean. We have been historically and culturally part of the Asia Pacific community for centuries. Today, with a renewed focus on the strategic importance of sea lanes of the Indian Ocean, maritime security is of vital importance to the entire Asia Pacific region.

Free, safe and secure sea lanes in the Indian Ocean region and beyond are vital to our interests in a globalising world. We depend on sea lanes of communications for flow of trade, energy and information. India's global mercantile trade has grown phenomenally and now constitutes 41 per cent of our GDP. 77 per cent of our trade by value and over 90 per cent by volume is carried by sea. The present maritime security environment faces a range of challenges, including piracy, smuggling, terrorism, transnational crimes, drug-trafficking and proliferation of sensitive items. The growing reach of piracy closer to our shores is posing new challenges to our security. In this environment, there is a need for expanding cooperative efforts to address these challenges effectively. India has, this week, assumed Chairmanship of the Indian Ocean Rim Association for Regional Cooperation (IOR-ARC). In this role, we look forward to contributing actively in enhancing cooperation in the region.

The pivot of our 'Look East' policy has been a deepening of our relations with ASEAN. Starting as a sectoral dialogue partner of ASEAN in 1992, India became a full dialogue partner of ASEAN in 1995. Since 2002, India and ASEAN have met annually at the Summit level. We look at ASEAN as an anchor for the stability of the Asia Pacific region. In our engagement with this region, we have stressed the central role played by ASEAN. We believe that the ASEAN approach of step-by-step and consensus-based process has its advantages and has worked well.

Mutually beneficial economic engagement has been the primary driver of India's engagement with the Asia Pacific region. We have concluded a Comprehensive Economic Partnership (CEP) with ASEAN, as well as a Free Trade Area Agreement for goods, we are actively negotiating a similar FTA for services. We believe that such linkages provide a sound basis for sustaining our economic engagement with ASEAN. Our immediate goal, announced at the last India-ASEAN Summit, is to reach the level of US$70 billion in two-way trade, by 2012.

As new countries have joined ASEAN over the past decade, we have been able to use our role as a dialogue partner to assist these new countries to integrate faster within the region. One of our major initiatives in this context has been the Mekong Ganga Cooperation initiative, established in November 2000 in Vientiane. The initiative brings together India, Myanmar, Thailand, Cambodia, Laos and Vietnam and seeks to develop linkages in the transportation, educational, tourism and cultural sectors to provide the foundations for trade and investment cooperation in the region.

The development of the emerging security architecture in the Asia Pacific region is a matter of interest and importance to India. We would like to see the evolution of a balanced, open and inclusive framework involving Asian countries and major non-Asian players. There is immense scope for the two major emerging economies of the Asia Pacific region, India and China, to engage in closer dialogue with each other. We share common concerns on issues of maritime security, the free flow of global trade through the Asia Pacific region and terrorism. We are in favour of a balanced and inclusive security architecture in our region, which includes India and China.

It is significant to note, against the backdrop of renewed fears of a global economic crisis, that six of the twenty members of the G-20, including India and China, belong to the East Asia Summit (EAS) process. In our view, the emergence of the EAS, since its first meeting in Kuala Lumpur in December 2005, has been a major development. The EAS has become an integral part of the regional architecture and a purposeful vehicle for community building in the region.

The EAS process has over the years grappled with immediate challenges such as disaster management, pandemics and energy security in 2007, the global economic crisis in 2008 and the climate change negotiations in 2009. The launching of the EAS process was an act of foresight. It was also an act of faith in our collective potential. We welcome the participation of the United States and Russia in the EAS.

We are committed to cooperating with ASEAN in ensuring pace, security, stability and development in the Asia Pacific region. It was in this context that India acceded to the Treaty of Amity and Cooperation (TAC) in South-East Asia in October 2003 during the 2nd ASEAN-India Summit in Bali. We also signed a Joint Declaration for Cooperation in Combating International Terrorism, recognising that in today's age, the destructive threat of terrorism poses a continuing threat to our shared vision of peaceful socio-economic development.

India is an active participant in the ASEAN Regional Forum (ARF), which was established in 1994. ARF has served as an important regional platform for dialogue and cooperation among its member states. The primary areas of cooperation are Disaster Relief, Maritime Security, Counter-Terrorism and Non-Proliferation and Disarmament. In the area of maritime security, the Indian Navy has been hosting the Milan series of biennial exercises since 1995 for building friendship and mutual understanding among participating navies of ARF countries. Cooperation and exchange of best practices on the maritime security issues were the core themes of Milan 2010, held at Port Blair in February 2010. In our view, the ARF is an important effort towards carving a pluralistic, cooperative security order in Asia, reflective of the unique diversity of the region. As the regional security architecture continues to evolve, it is important that the experience generated and capacity-building efforts undertaken under ARF over the last seventeen years are made use of in an optimal manner.

I would like to refer to India's participation in the ASEAN Defence Ministers Meeting Plus or ADMM Plus Eight process. The ADMM was mandated by the ASEAN Summit in 2003 to conceptualise an Asian Security

Community. The guiding principles of this process were articulated at the inaugural meeting of the ADMM in 2006, which encouraged ASEAN's cooperation with its dialogue partners through the 'Plus' mechanism. India is actively engaged in the ADMM Plus Eight process in five identified areas – humanitarian assistance and disaster relief, maritime security, military medicine, counter-terrorism and peacekeeping operations. Our common interest in participating in this process is to enhance regional peace and stability through cooperation in defence and security, in view of the transnational security challenges that the region faces.

Let me say a few words about India's relations with Japan with which we share a Strategic & Global Partnership. India is the largest recipient nation of Japanese Official Development Assistance or ODA for 8 years in a row. Japan has contributed enormously to infrastructure development in India. A good example is the Delhi Metro Project which commenced as a Japanese funded project. It has brought benefits to millions of residents of the National Capital Region. Similarly, Japan assists India in other projects such as the Dedicated Freight Corridor and Delhi Mumbai Industrial Corridor. Corporate Japan is looking at India much more seriously as an investment destination which is critical to our plans to ensure fast paced but equitable and inclusive growth. Japan's bullet train technology may be the next big idea in India-Japan economic cooperation, which brings together the 2nd and 3rd largest economies in Asia.

India's security cooperation with Japan has also witnessed a continuing upturn. Japan is the only country with which we have a 2+2 dialogue at the Secretary or Vice Minister level. We have expanded our Navy-to-Navy ties with joint bilateral as well as multilateral exercises. We have annual Defence and Foreign Minister level discussions. We have an Annual Summit of our Prime Ministers alternately in Delhi and Tokyo. We look forward to receiving Prime Minister Noda in India, later in 2011.

Regarding India China relations, we do not view our ties with China in any kind of antagonistic construct. We believe that there is sufficient space in the world for the rice of India, the rice of China as well as the rice of other countries in the region and beyond. As with China, we are witnessing record rates of growth. China is one of our largest trading partners. India welcomes this development and actively seeks greater investment from Chinese firms. Similarly, there are many Indian companies which are active in China including our software majors. Naturally, as with any two major nations, relations between India and China contain elements of cooperation as well as some elements of competition. This is not so surprising for two large neighbouring countries. The fact is that we have handled our relations with great dexterity over these past decades to ensure that we continue to build on the convergences between us while managing our differences. It is true that we have an unresolved Boundary Question, but at the same time we have ensured that peace and tranquility prevail in the India-China border areas. This provides us with the necessary condition for discussing our differences on the boundary in the Special Representatives format. However, China's rapid military modernisation, along with the new infrastructure she is creating in Tibet and Sinkiang across our borders, concerns us. A measured but corresponding response from India has been initiated so that we are able to ensure mutual and equal security for our own citizens. There is no justification for viewing these measures as being an impediment to our efforts to maintain the peace and tranquility in the India – China border areas. To sum up, India will continue her engagement with China on the basis of equality and mutual benefit and sensitivity to each others concerns.

From this overview, it emerges that India's interest and participation in the evolving economic and security structures of the Asia Pacific region is significant. In December 2012, we will be marking the 20th anniversary of the establishment of our first dialogue relationship with ASEAN, by hosting a Commemorative India-ASEAN Summit in India. It is my hope that your deliberations at this Seminar will be made available as a very useful input into our preparations for this historic event.

VOTE OF THANKS

Lieutenant General PK Singh, PVSM, AVSM (Retd) Director, USI

I thank you for coming to the Seminar and delivering the Valedictory address. I extend my sincere thanks to the participants of the Seminar, who have been with us for the last two days. I also thank the young diplomats who are attending a course with the Foreign Services Institute for attending the Seminar. It was very kind of you to be here for the last two days. Your presence added to the benefit of the Conference. I would like to tell my friends, participants of the foreign countries and everyone present that the next year's NSS will be held on the 22nd and 23rd of November 2012. Please block these dates on your calendar. We will be writing to you very shortly with the suggested theme and I shall send a special copy to my dear friend Dr Michael Pillsbury. I invite all to participate in next year's conference. I would request everyone present to please join me in giving a big hand to our participants, who made these two days interesting and informative.